I0446899

FRANCE STOREFRONT
Coloring Book

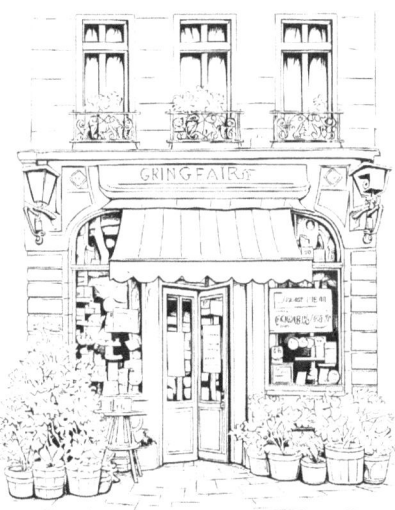

Step into the enchanting world of France with the " France Storefront Coloring Book."
This unique coloring book offers 50 illustrations of diverse France storefronts on
single-sided pages, providing a delightful journey through the captivating charm of
traditional France architecture and the vibrant culture it represents. Immerse yourself in
art of coloring as you bring these beautiful storefronts to life with your creativity.

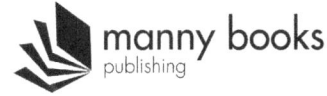
manny books
publishing

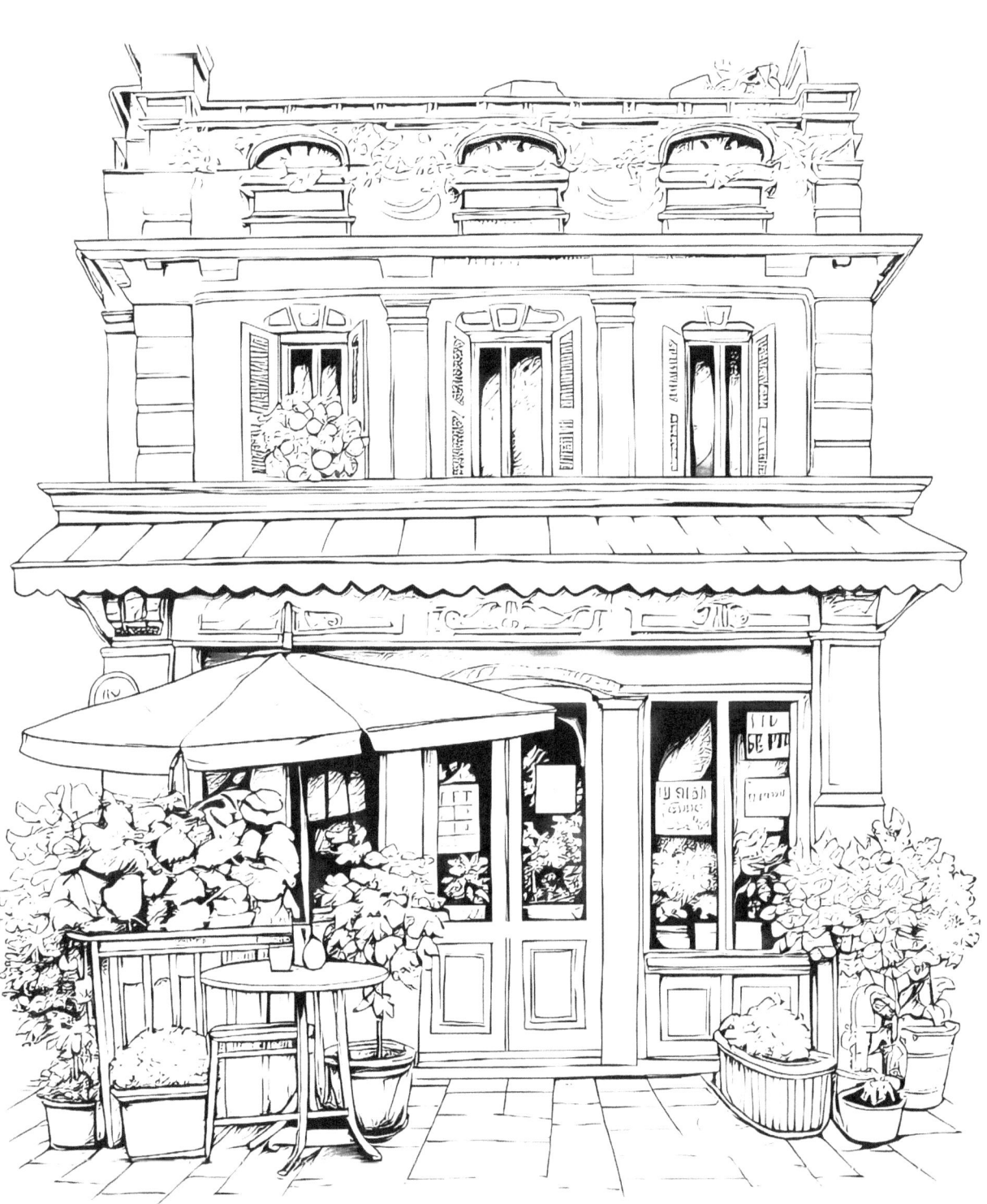

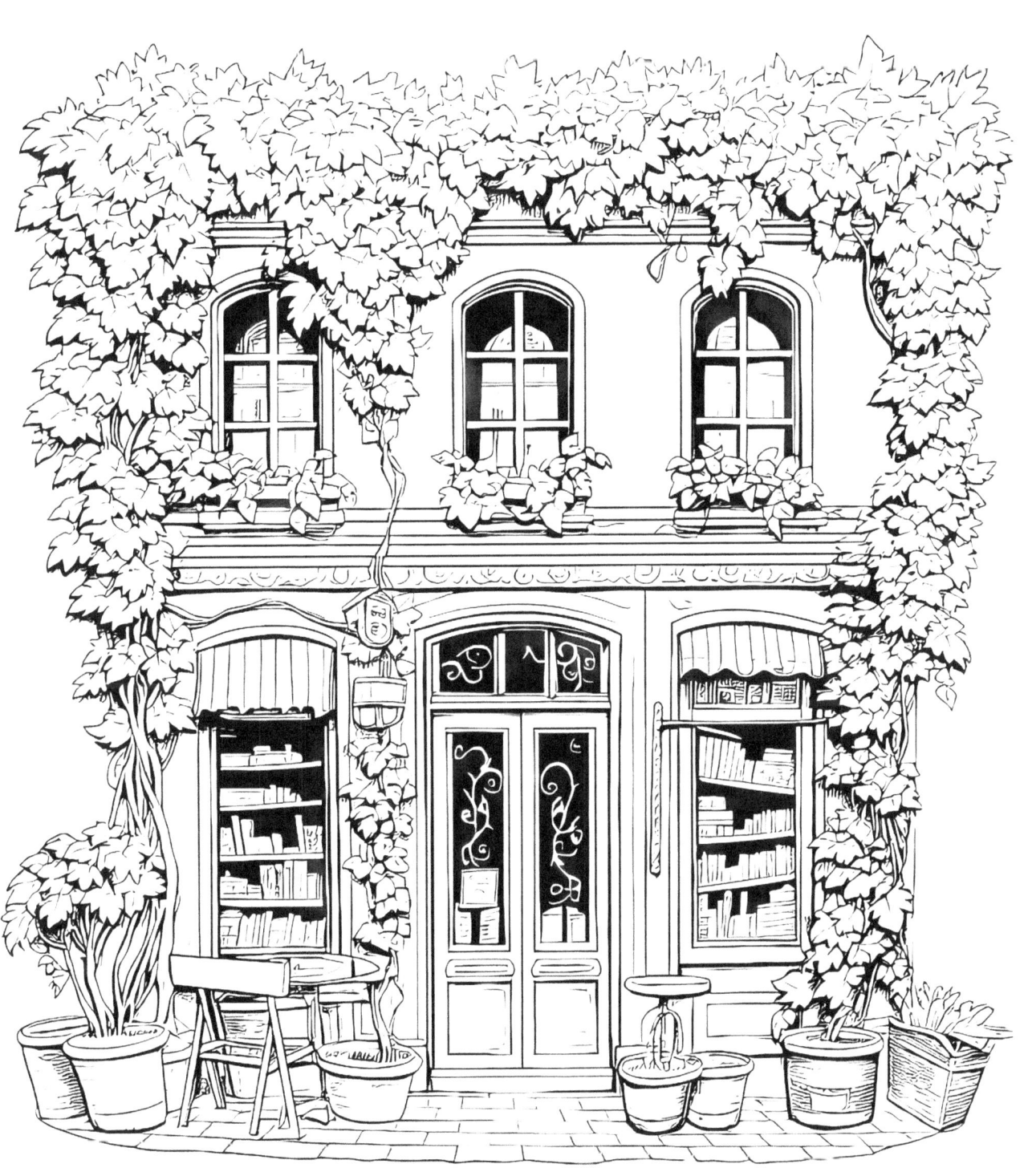

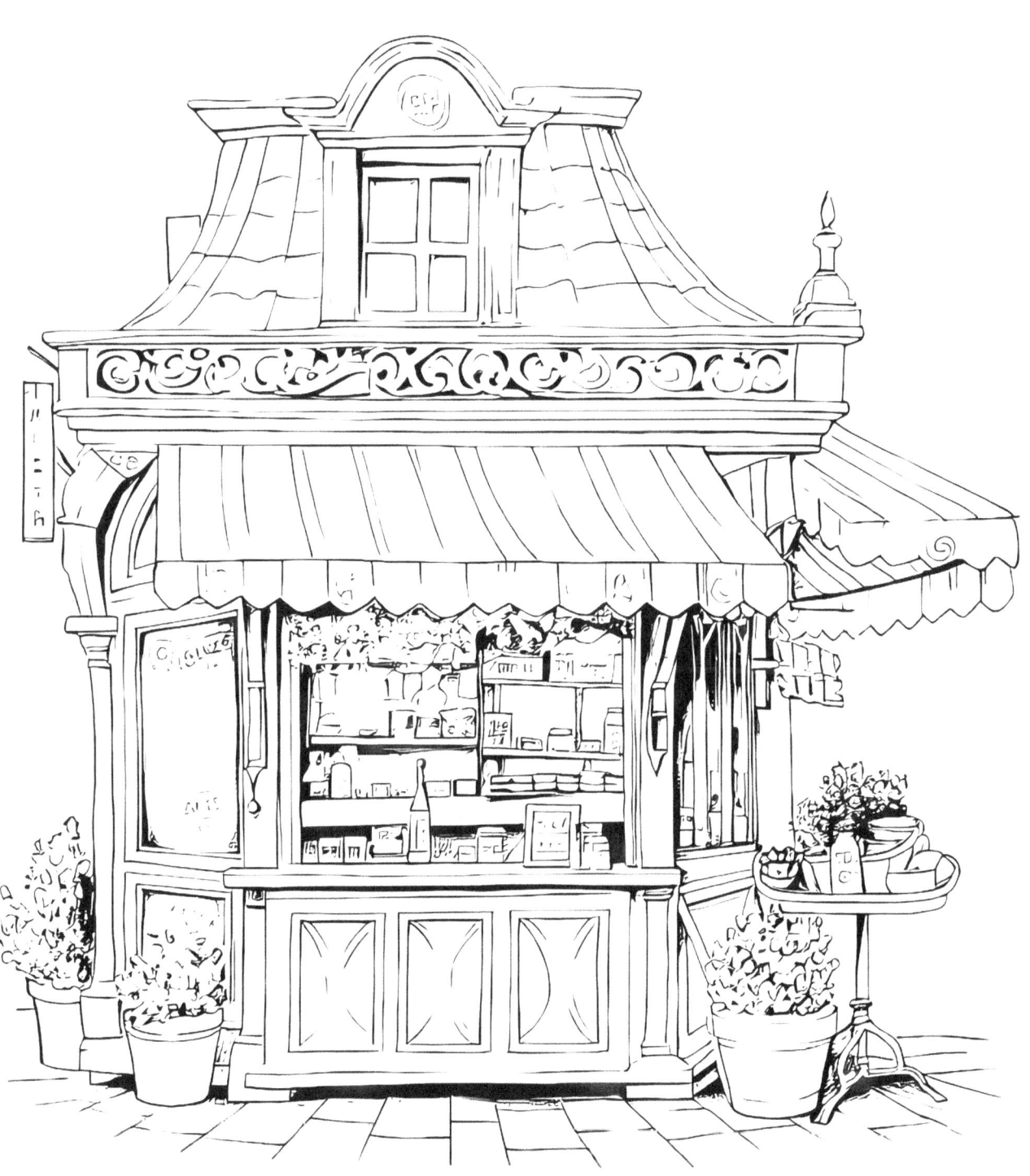

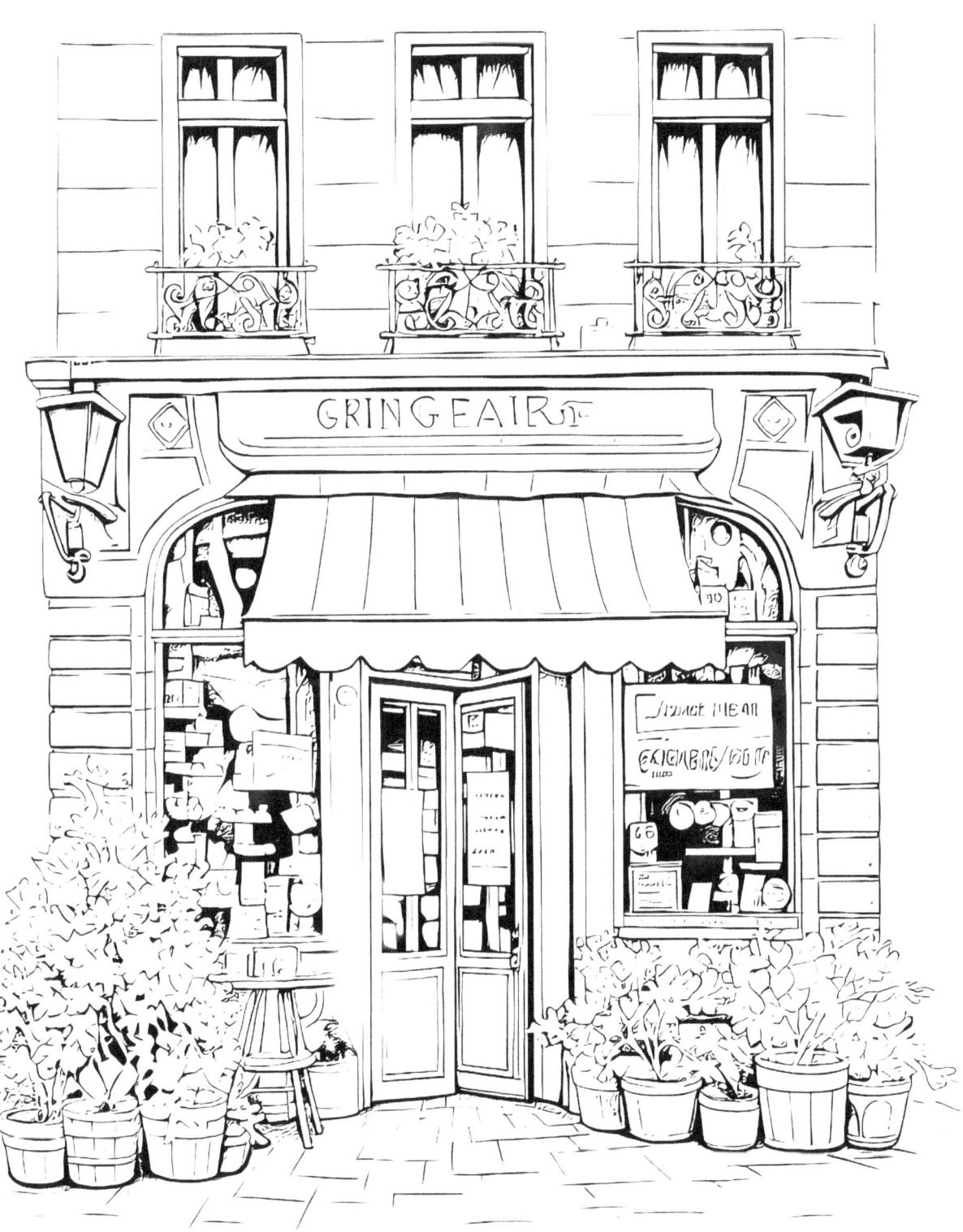

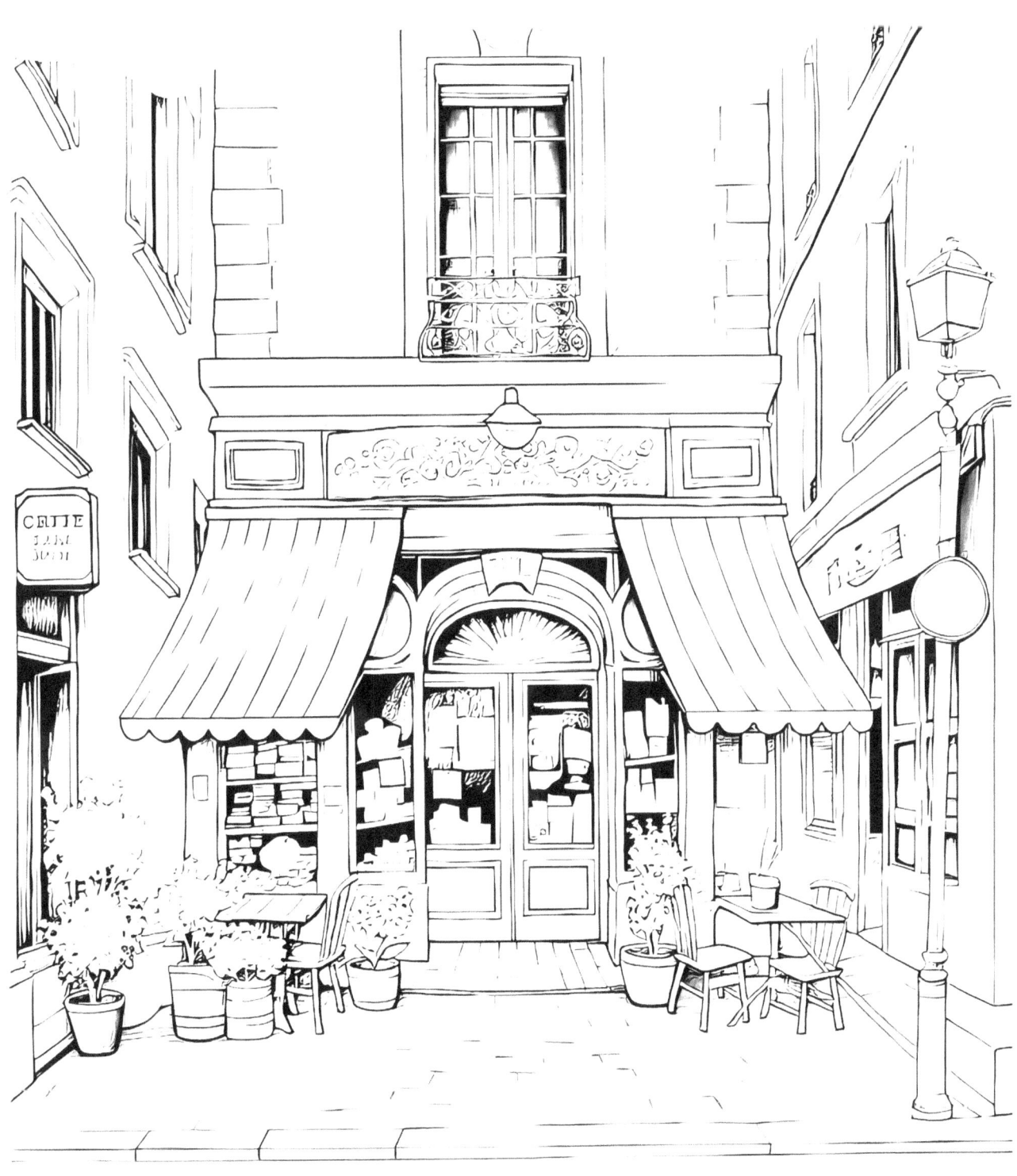

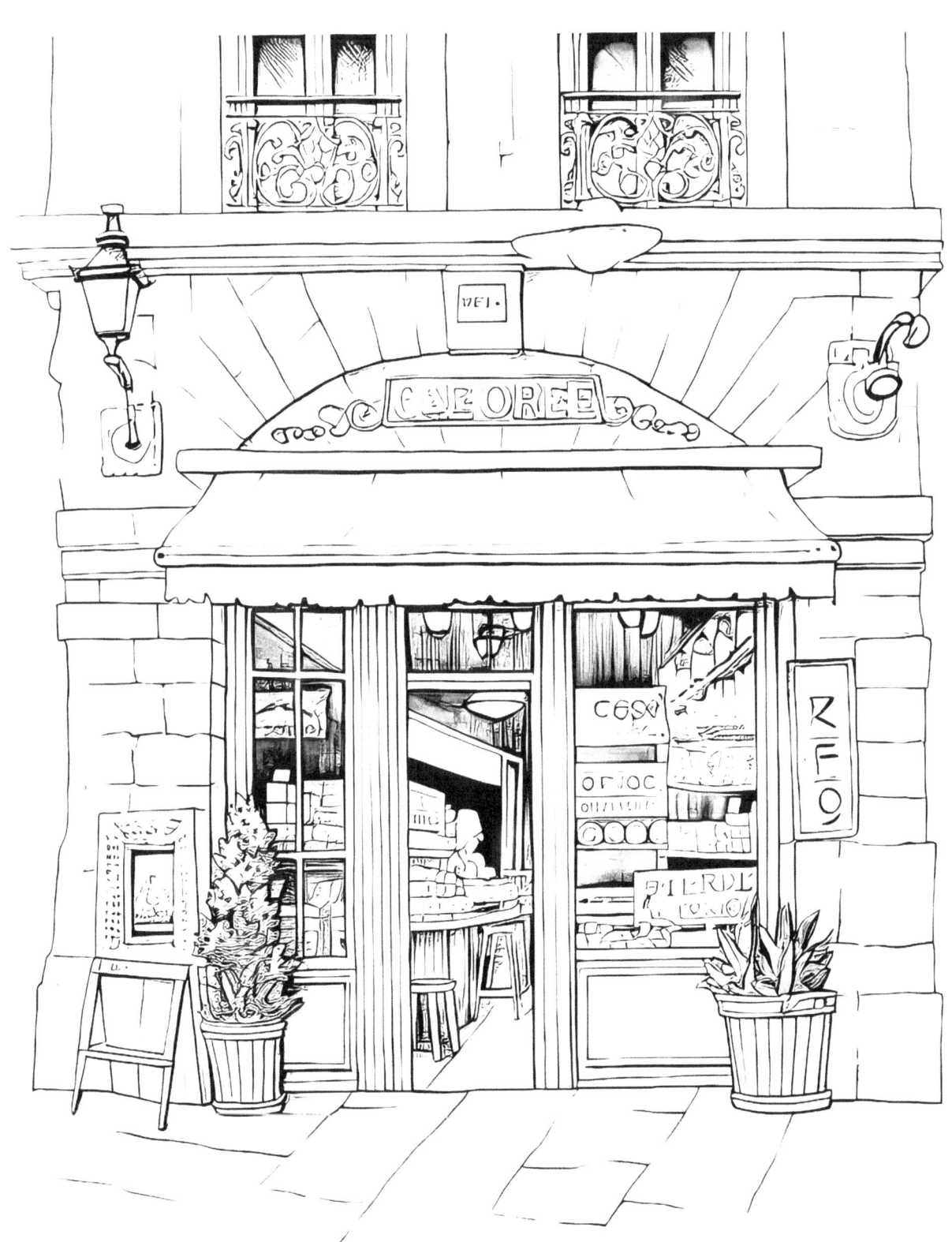

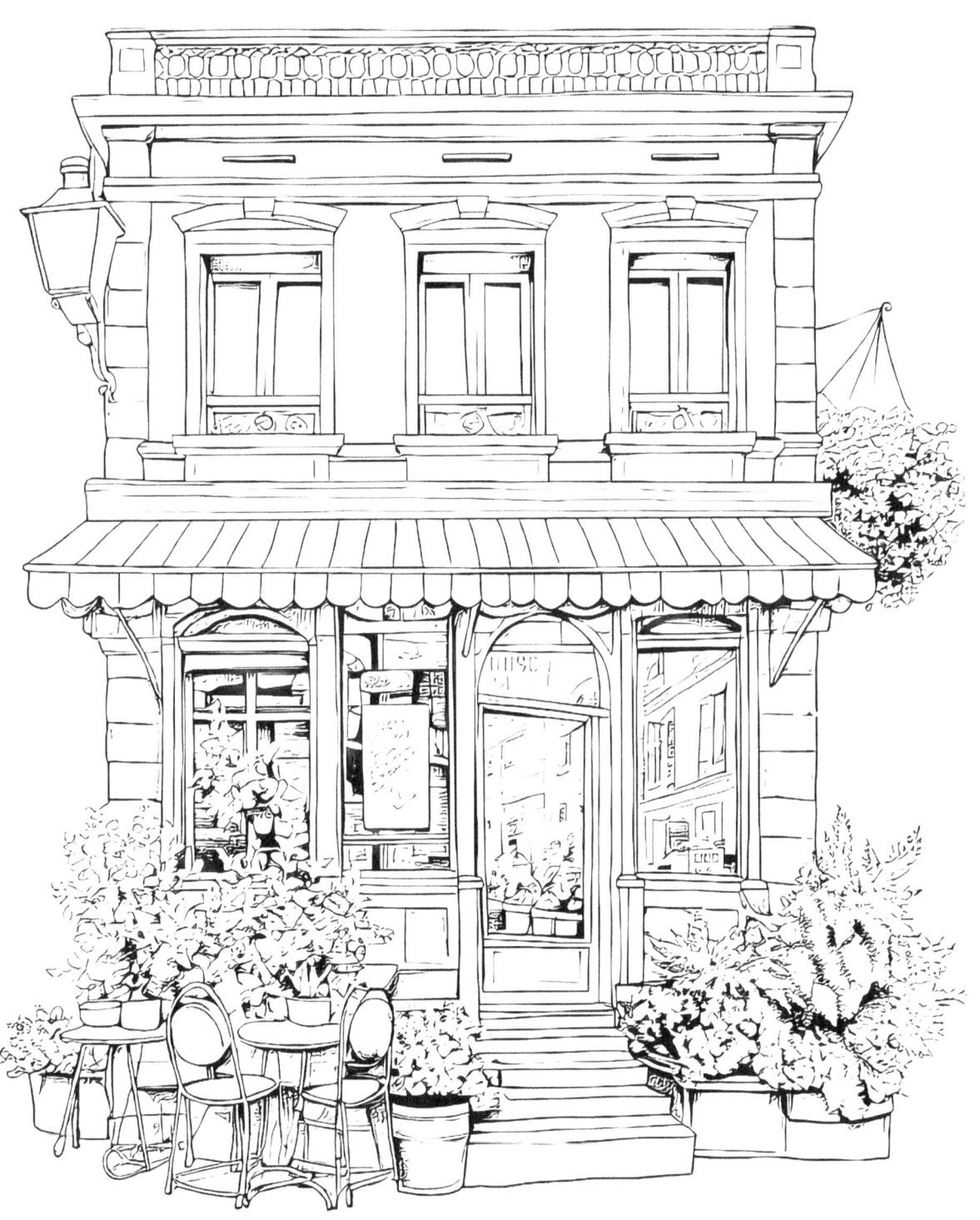

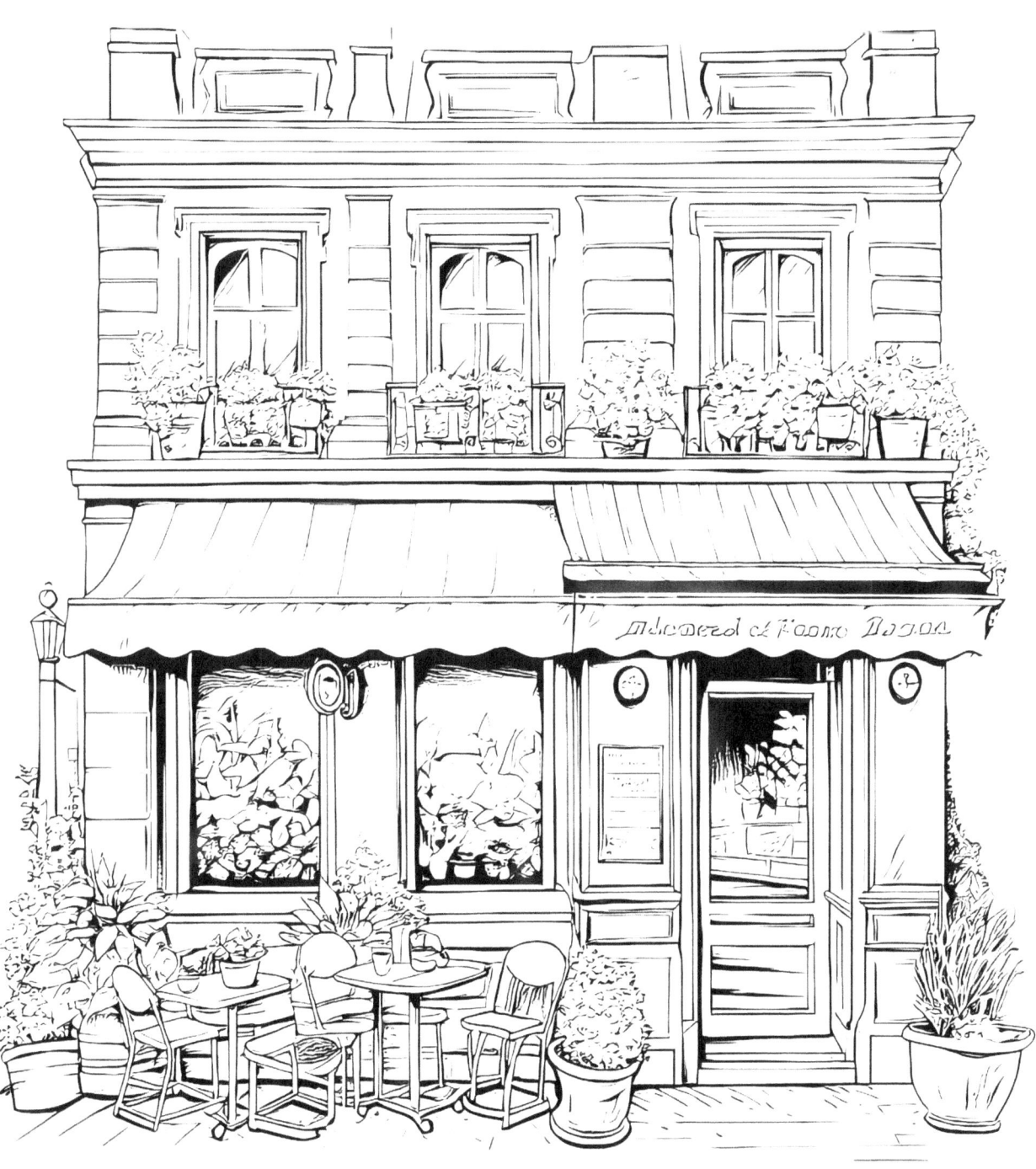

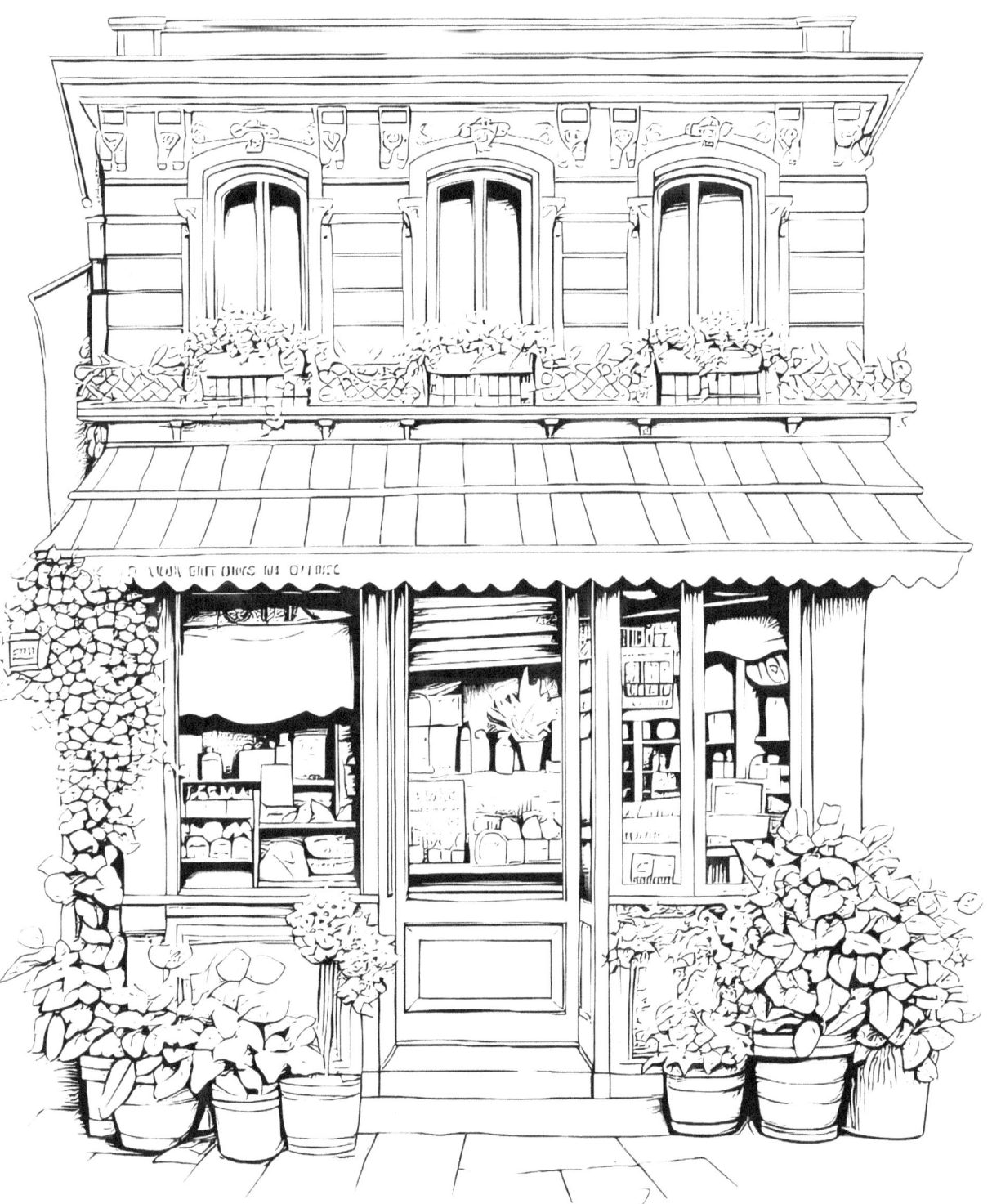

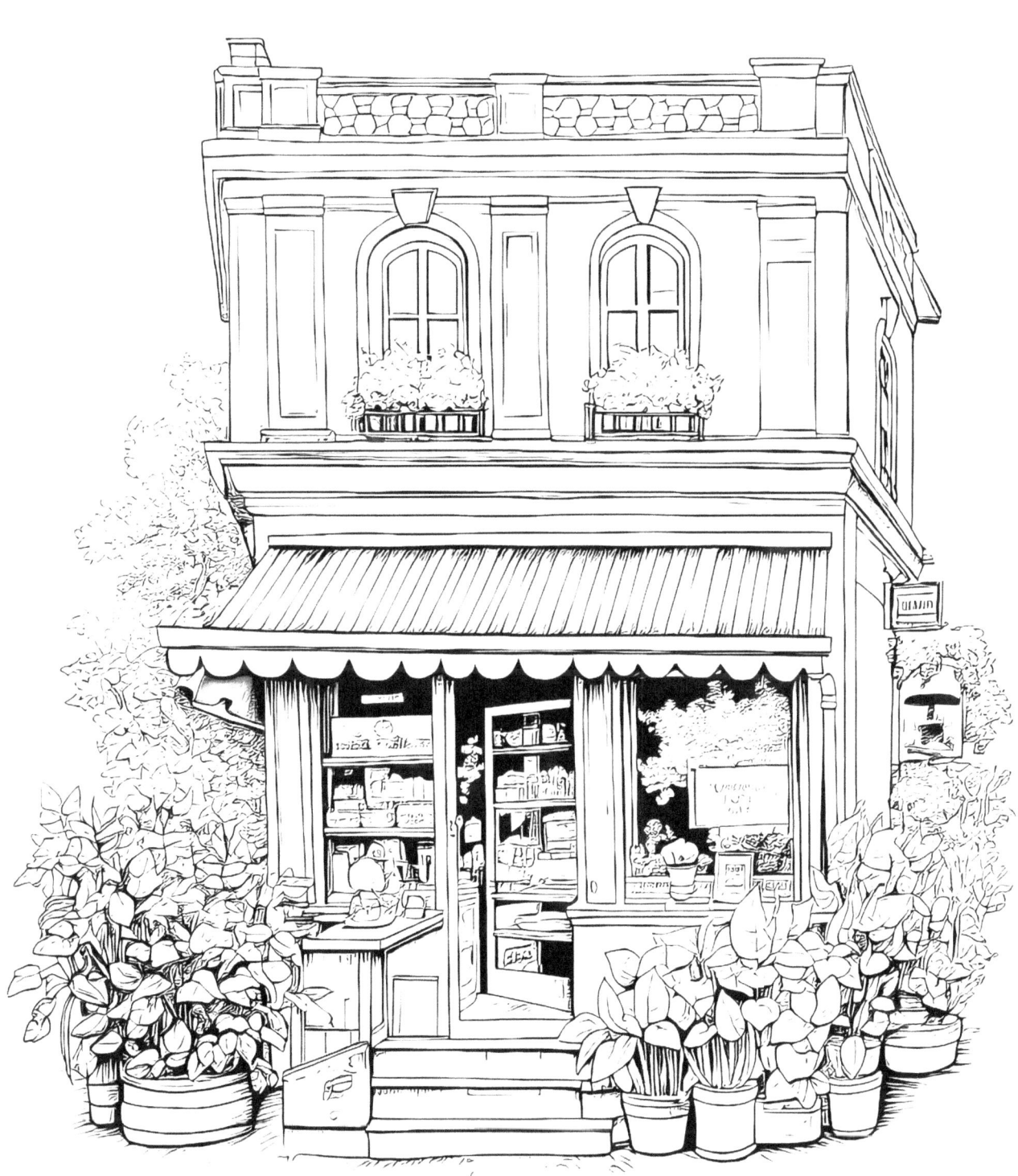

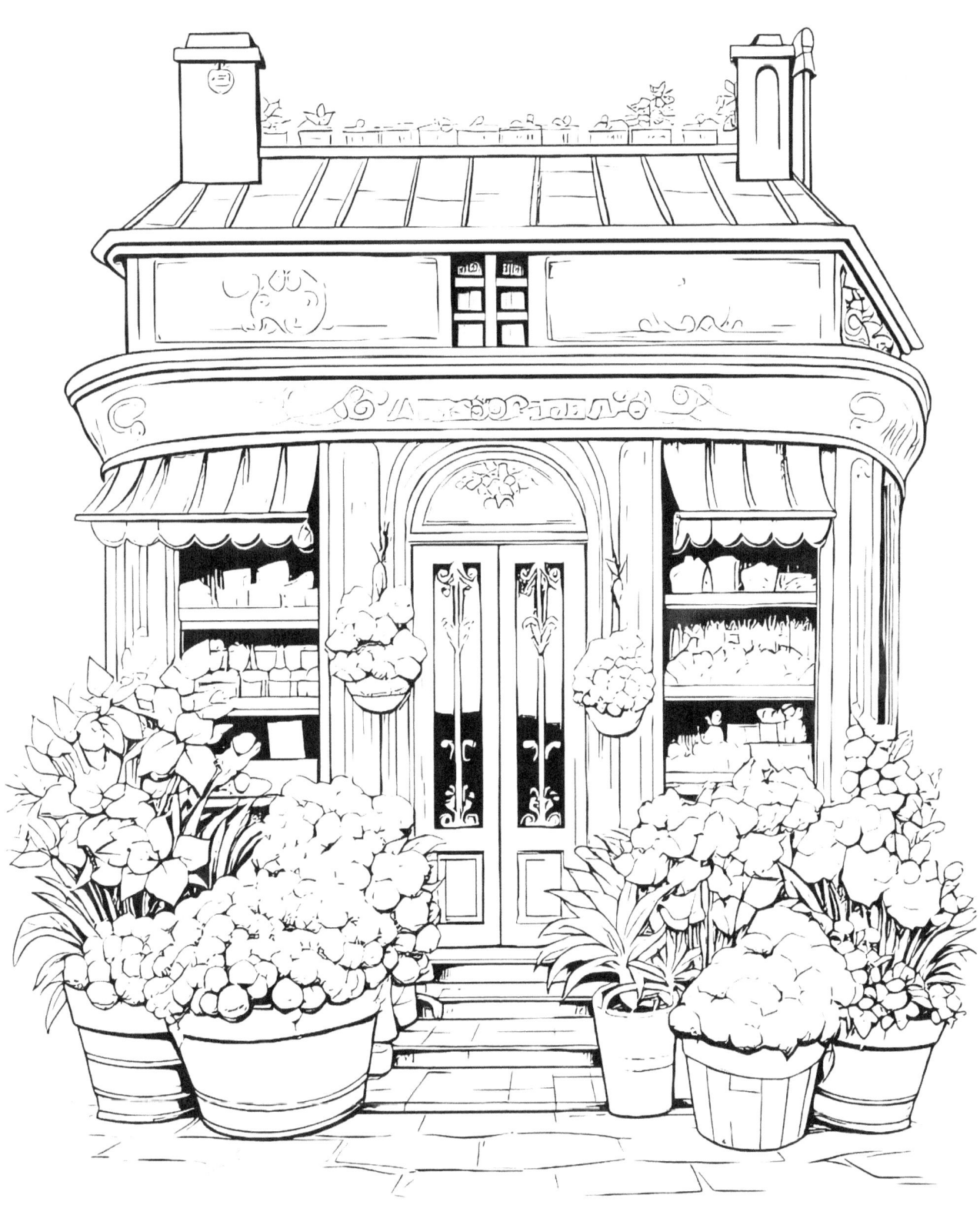

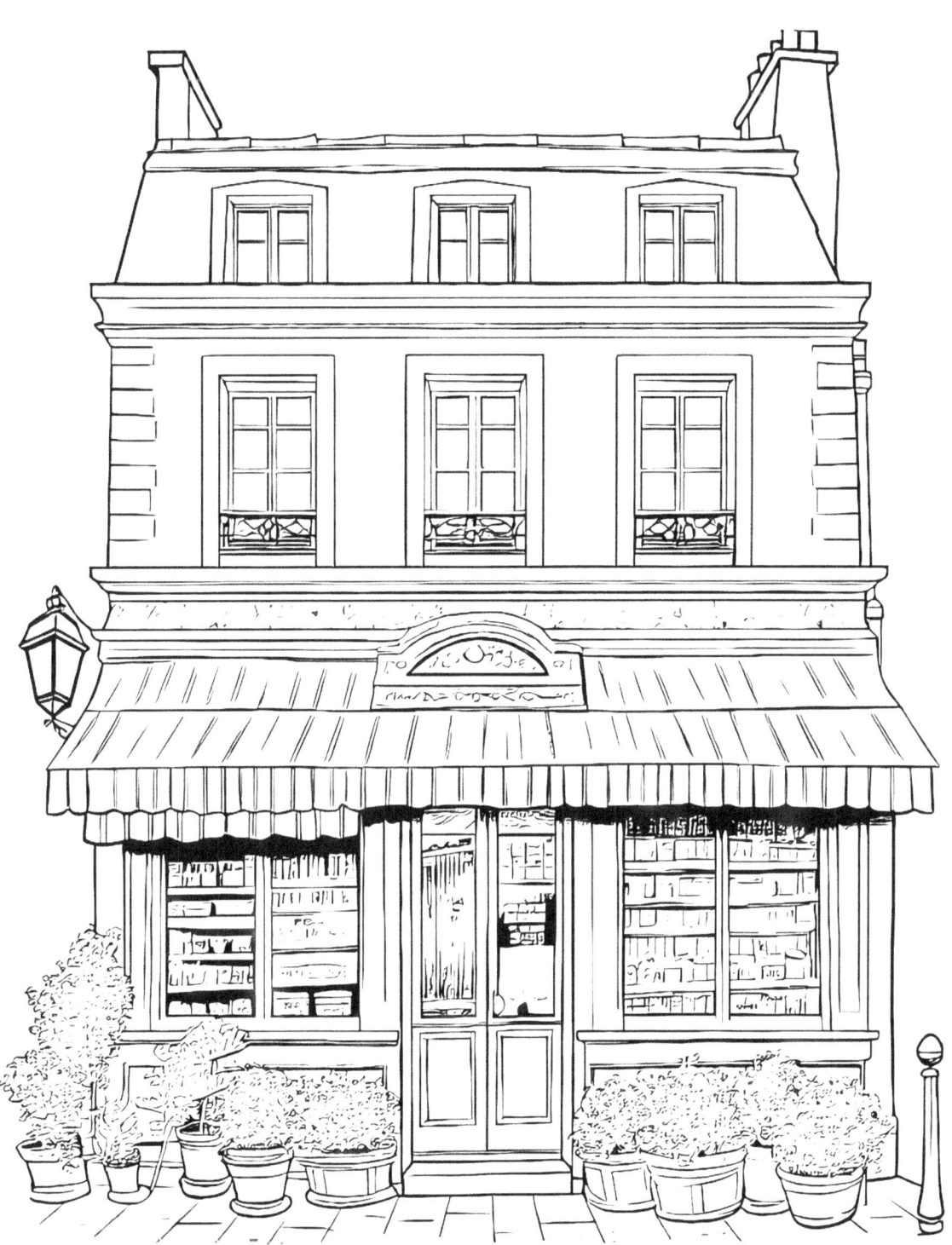

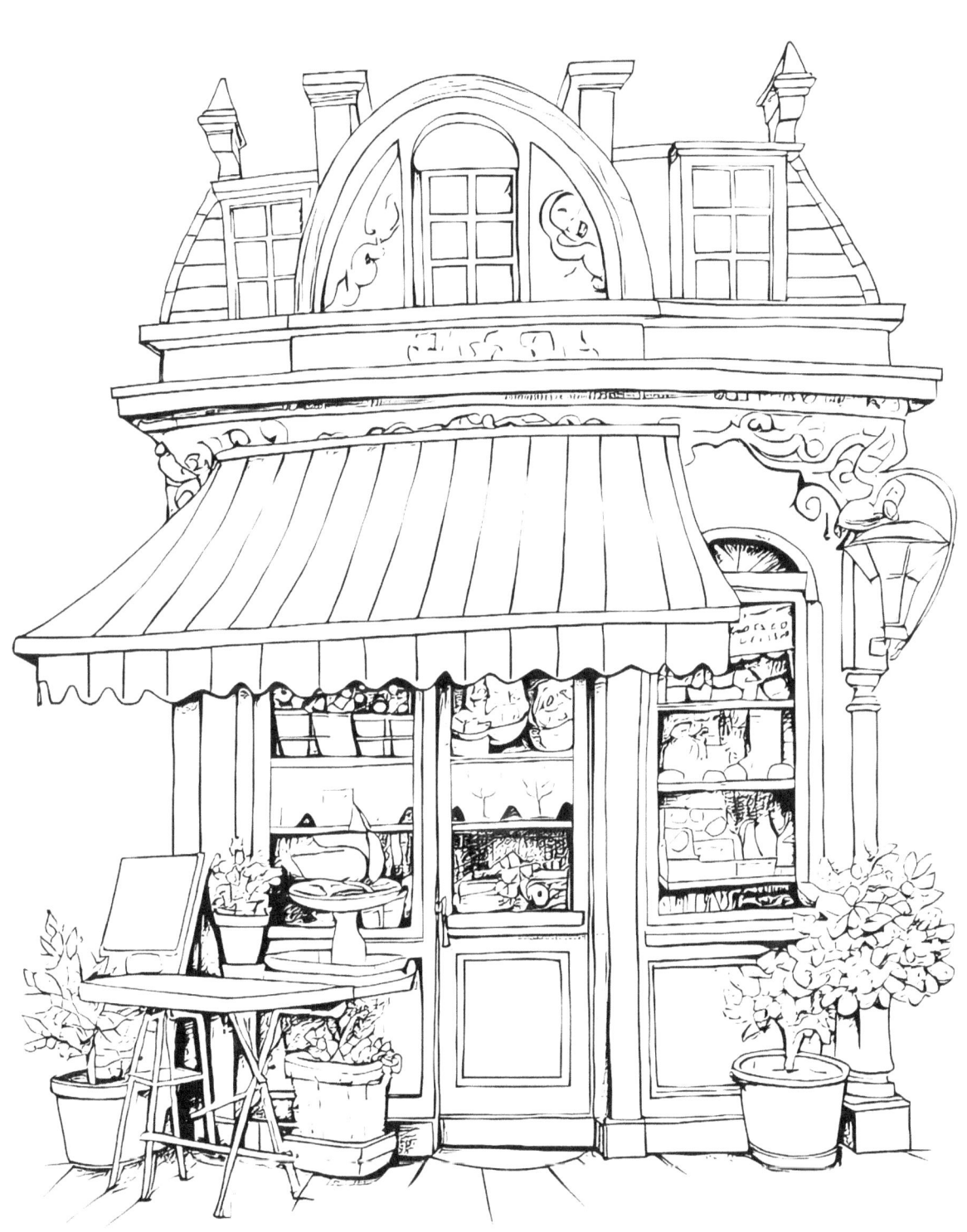

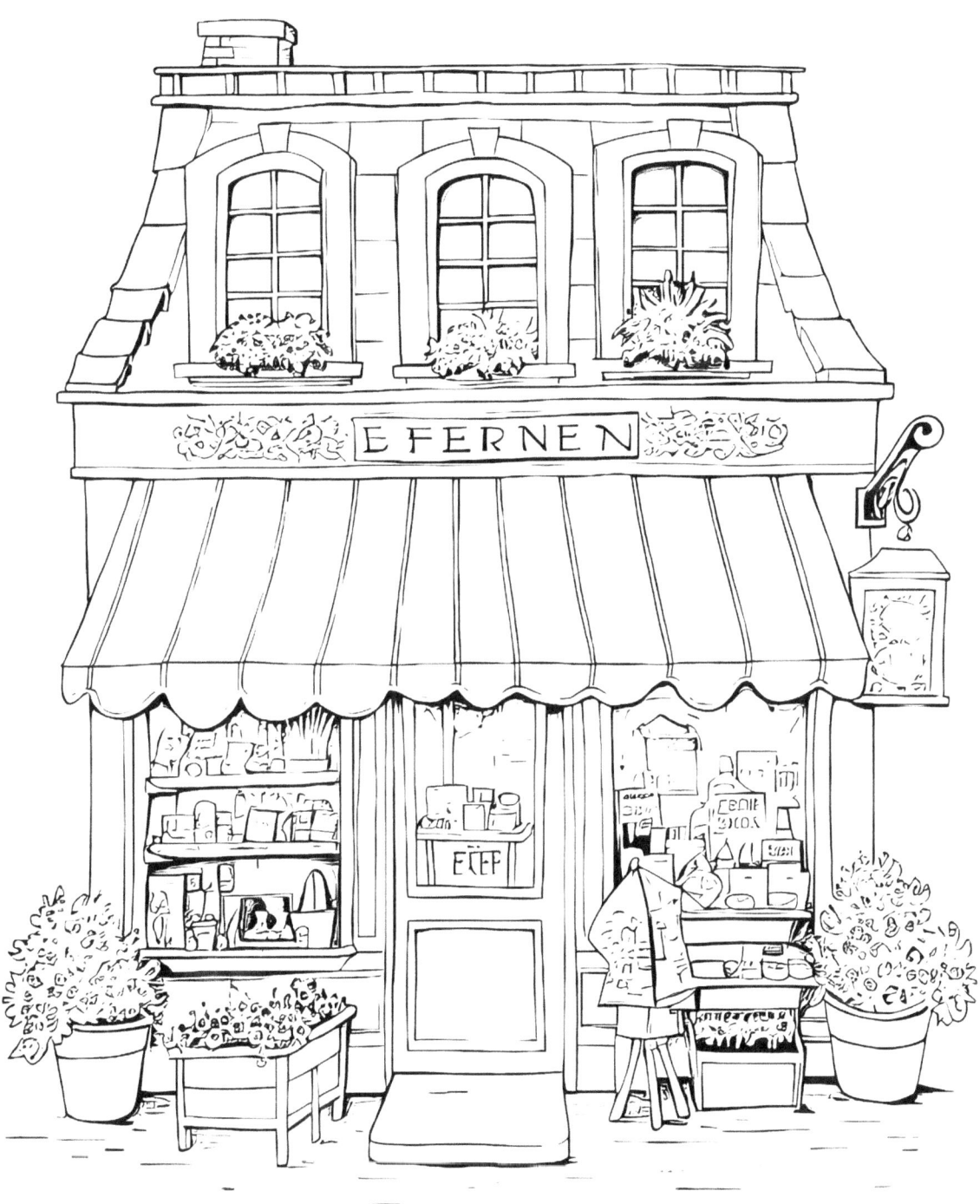

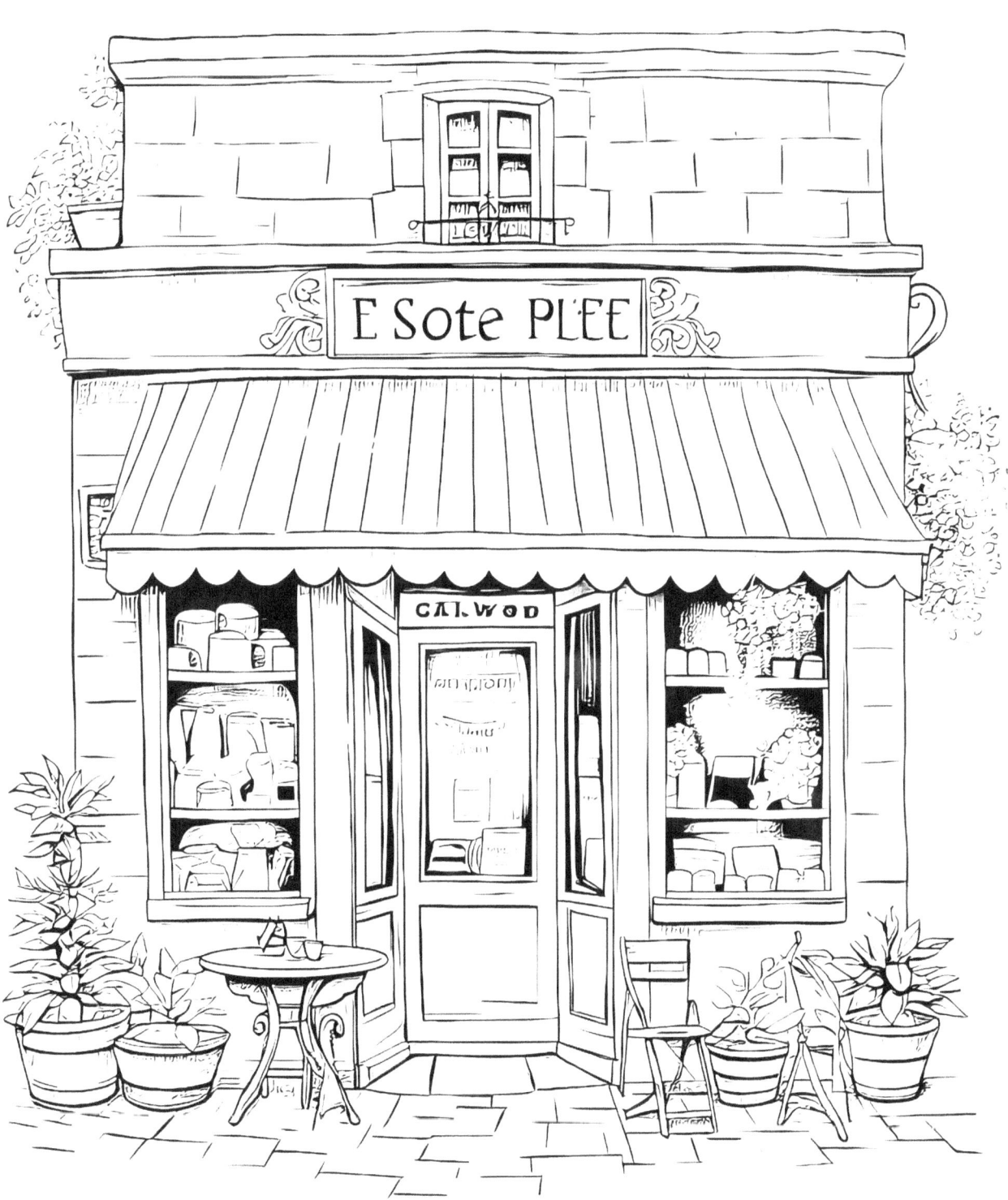

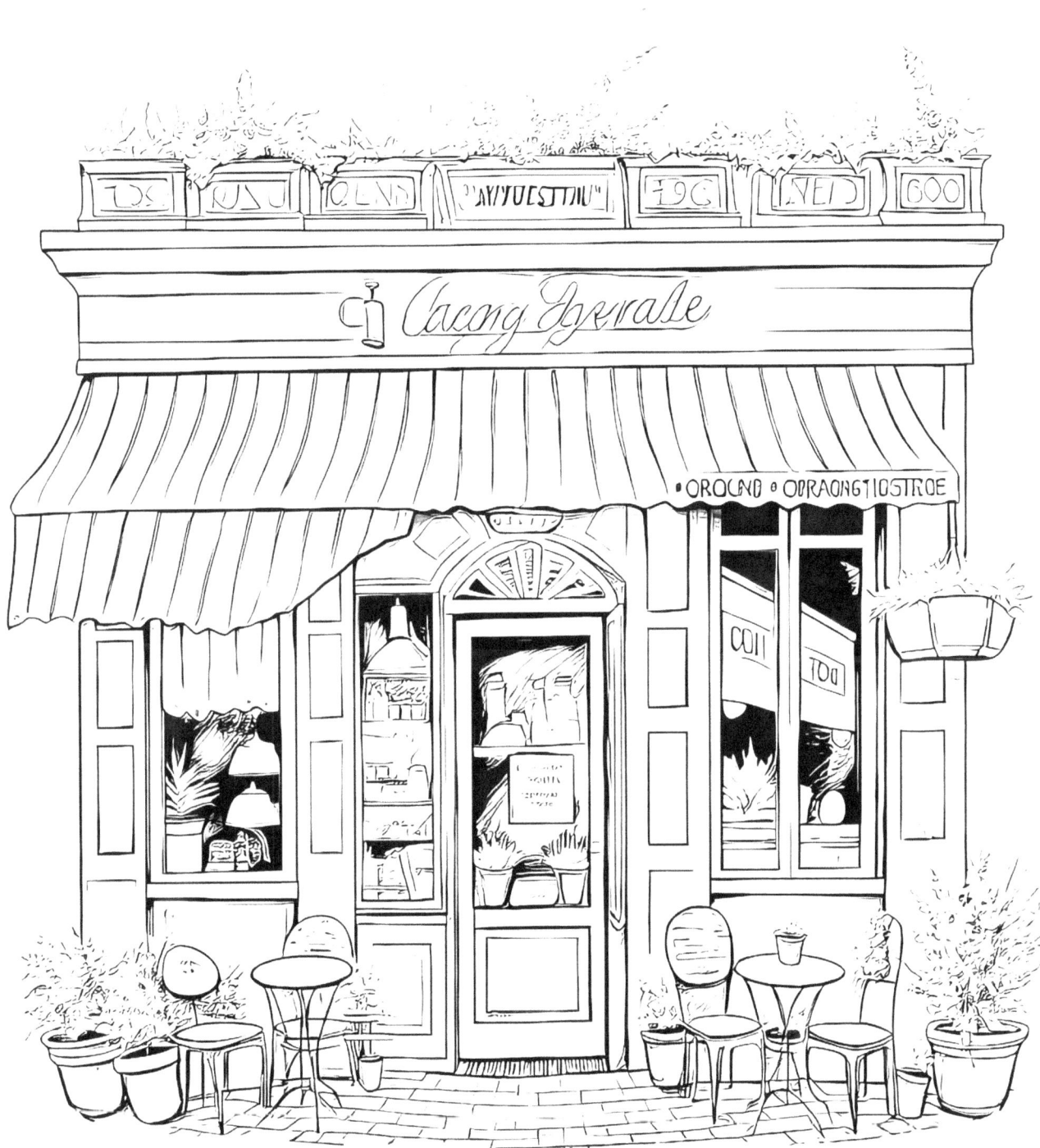

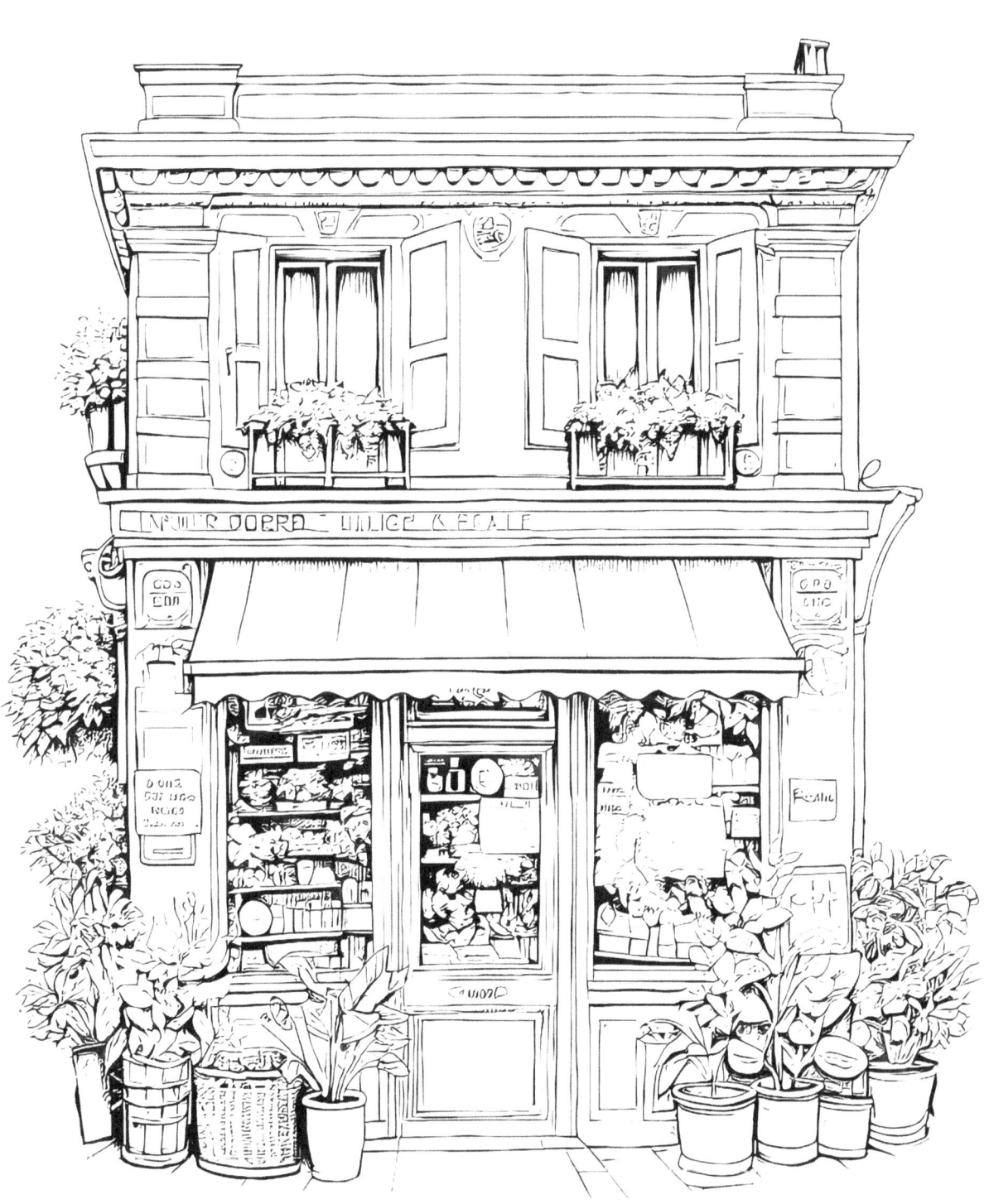

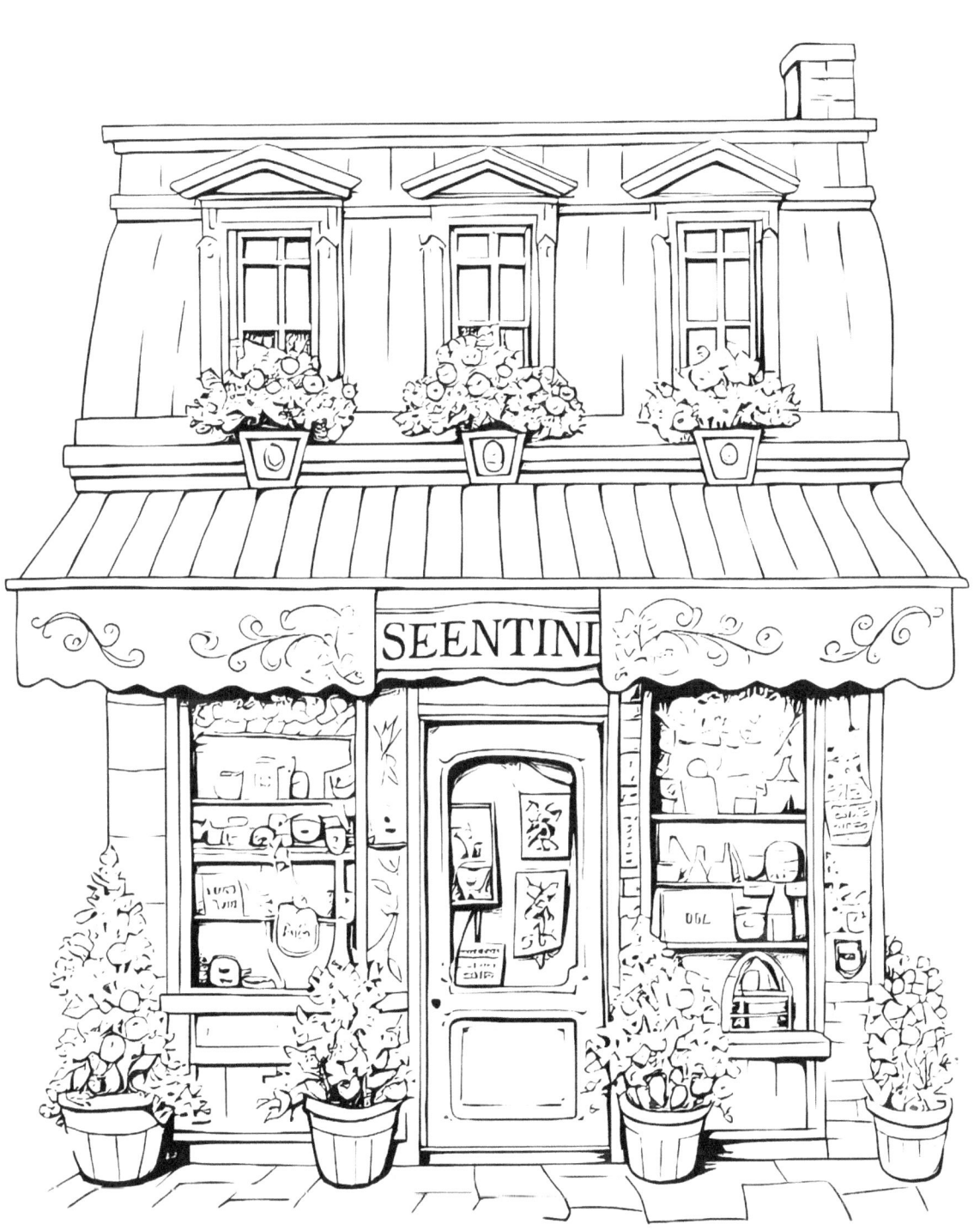

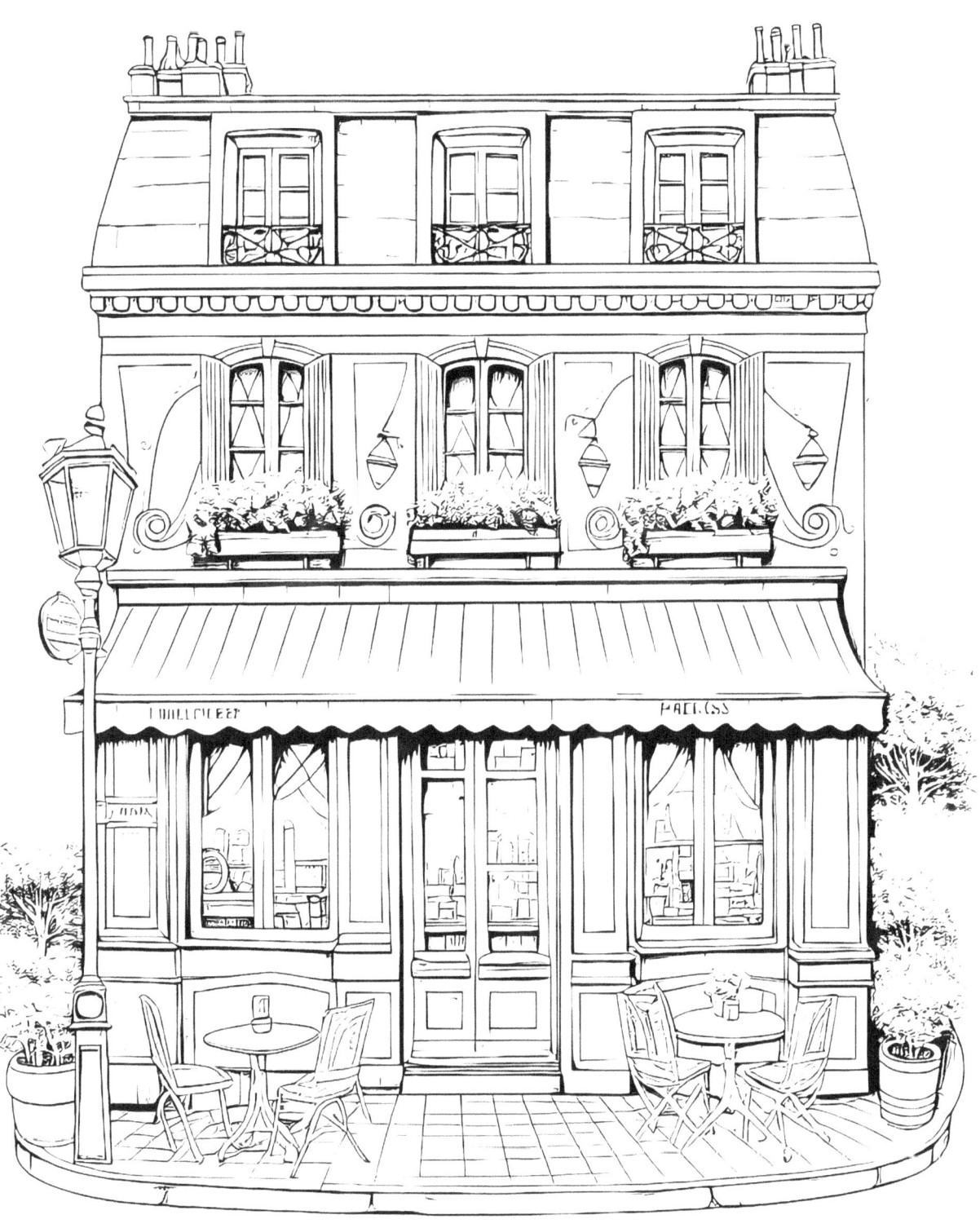

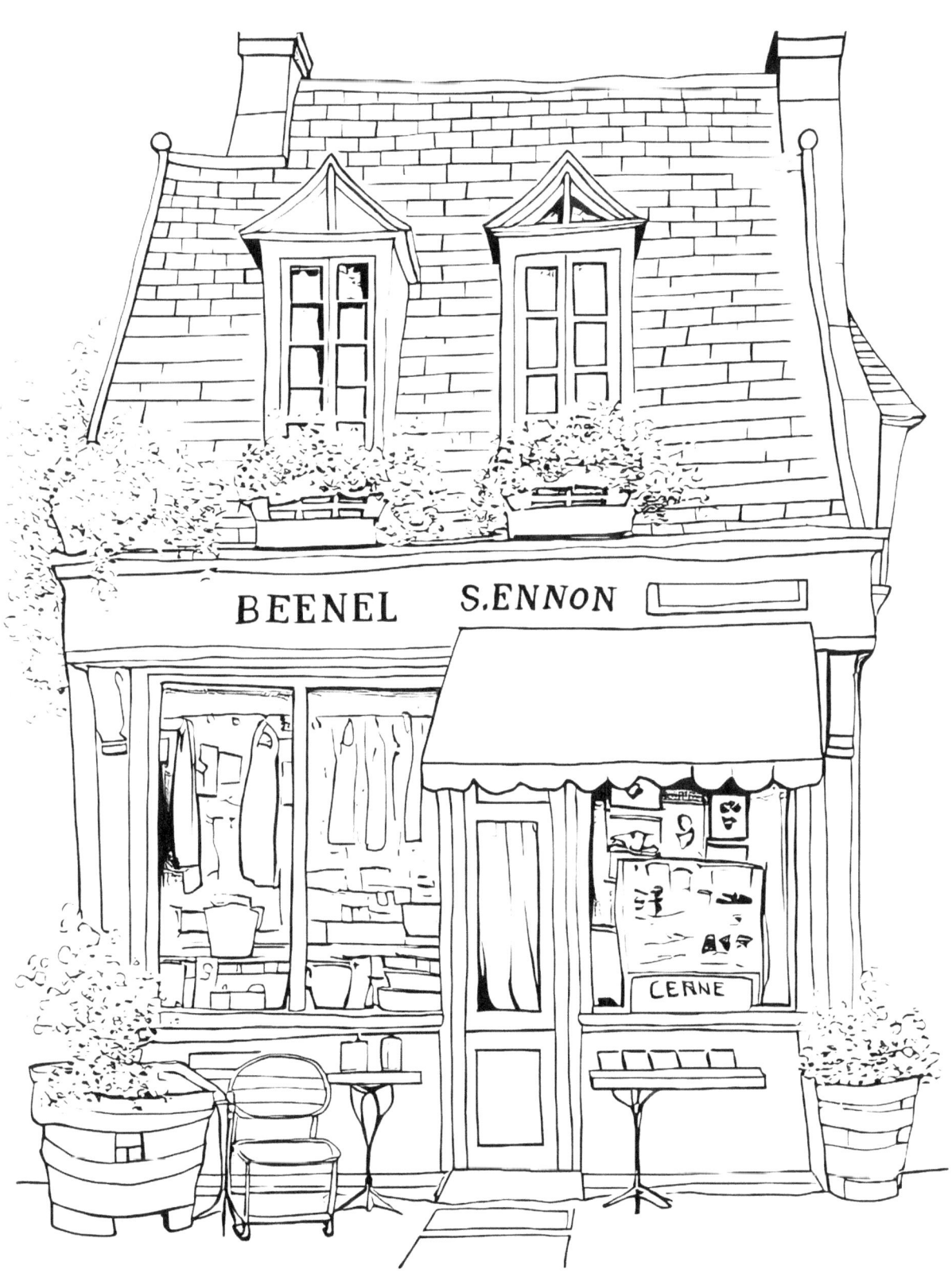

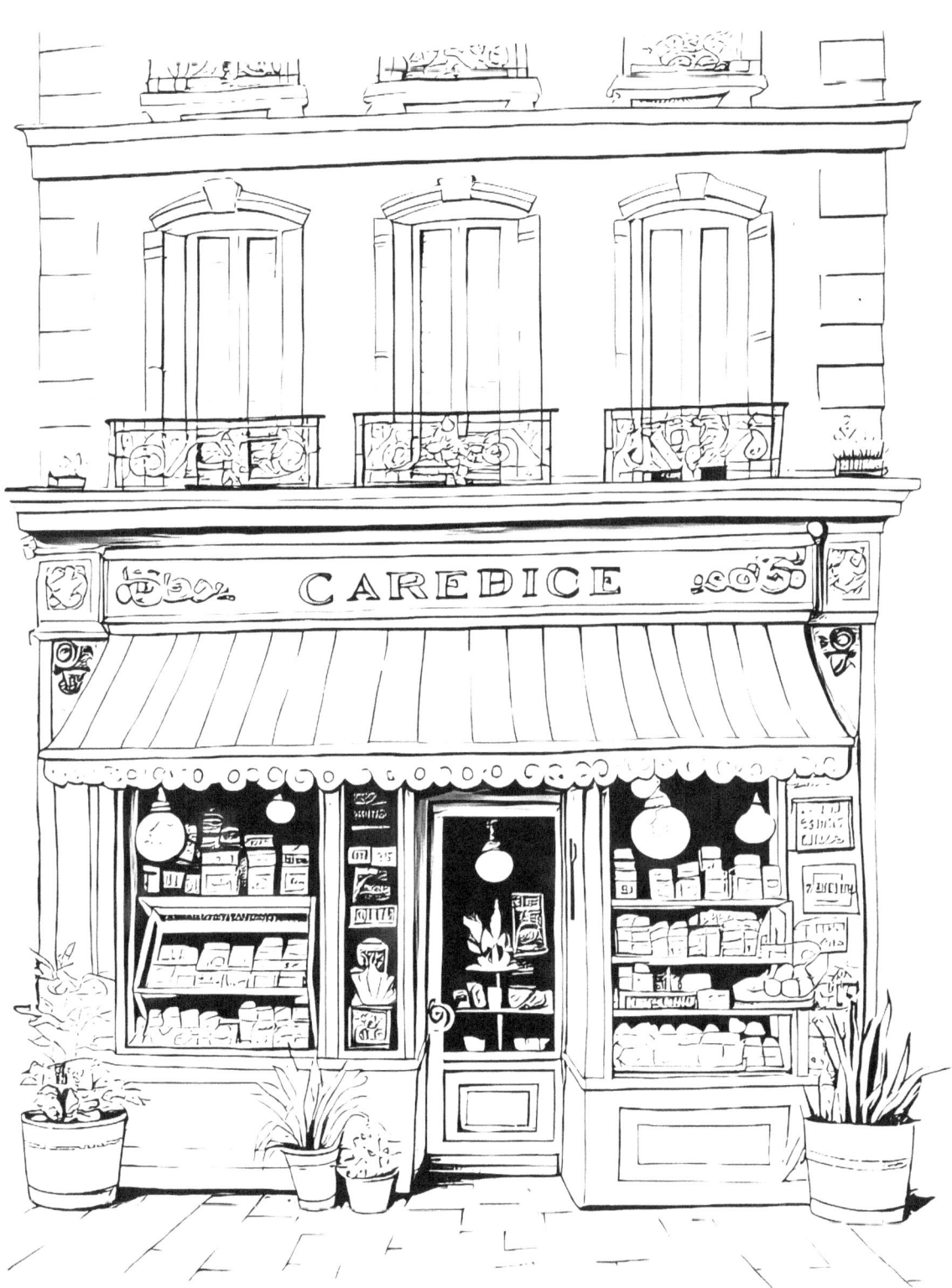

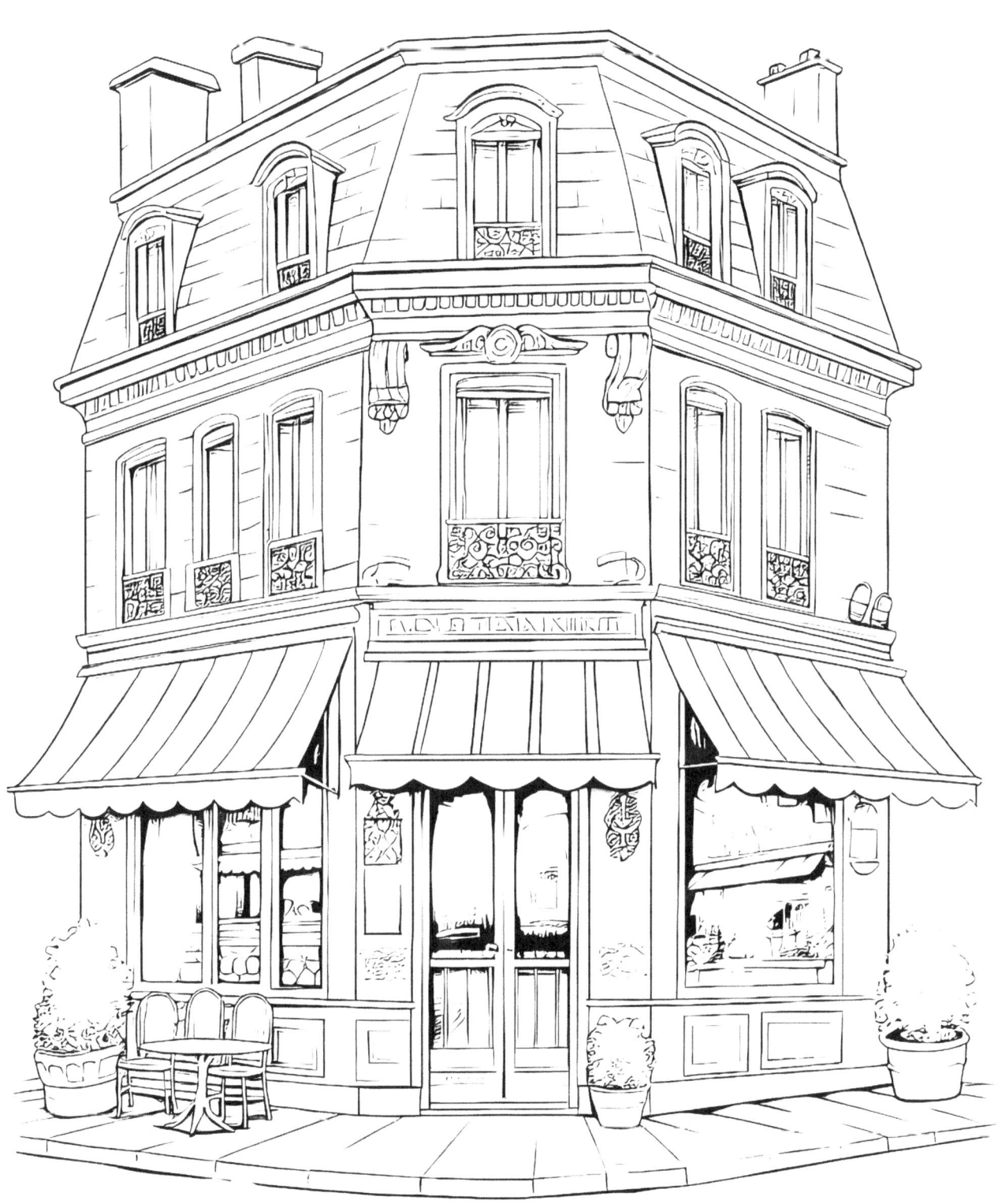

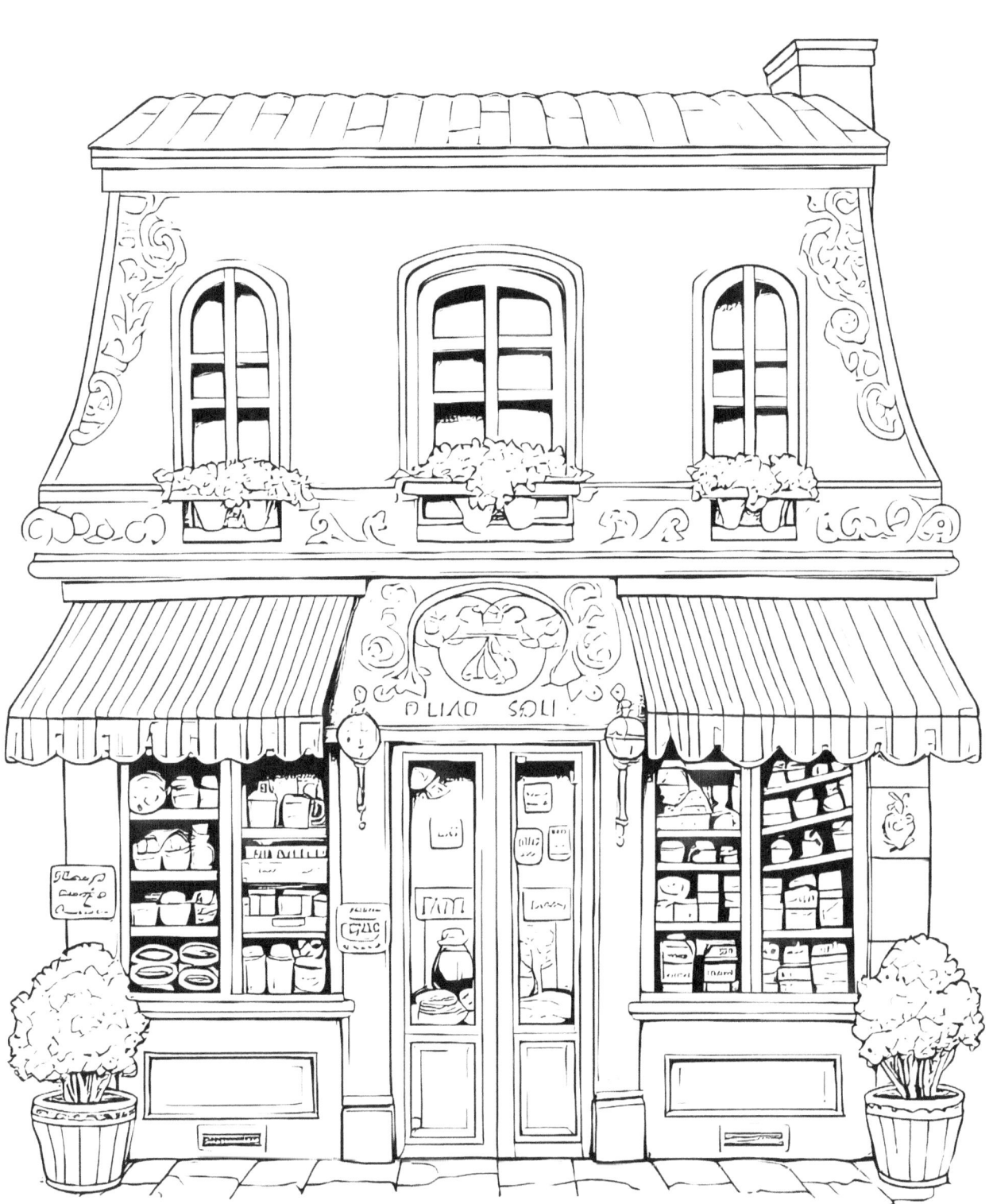

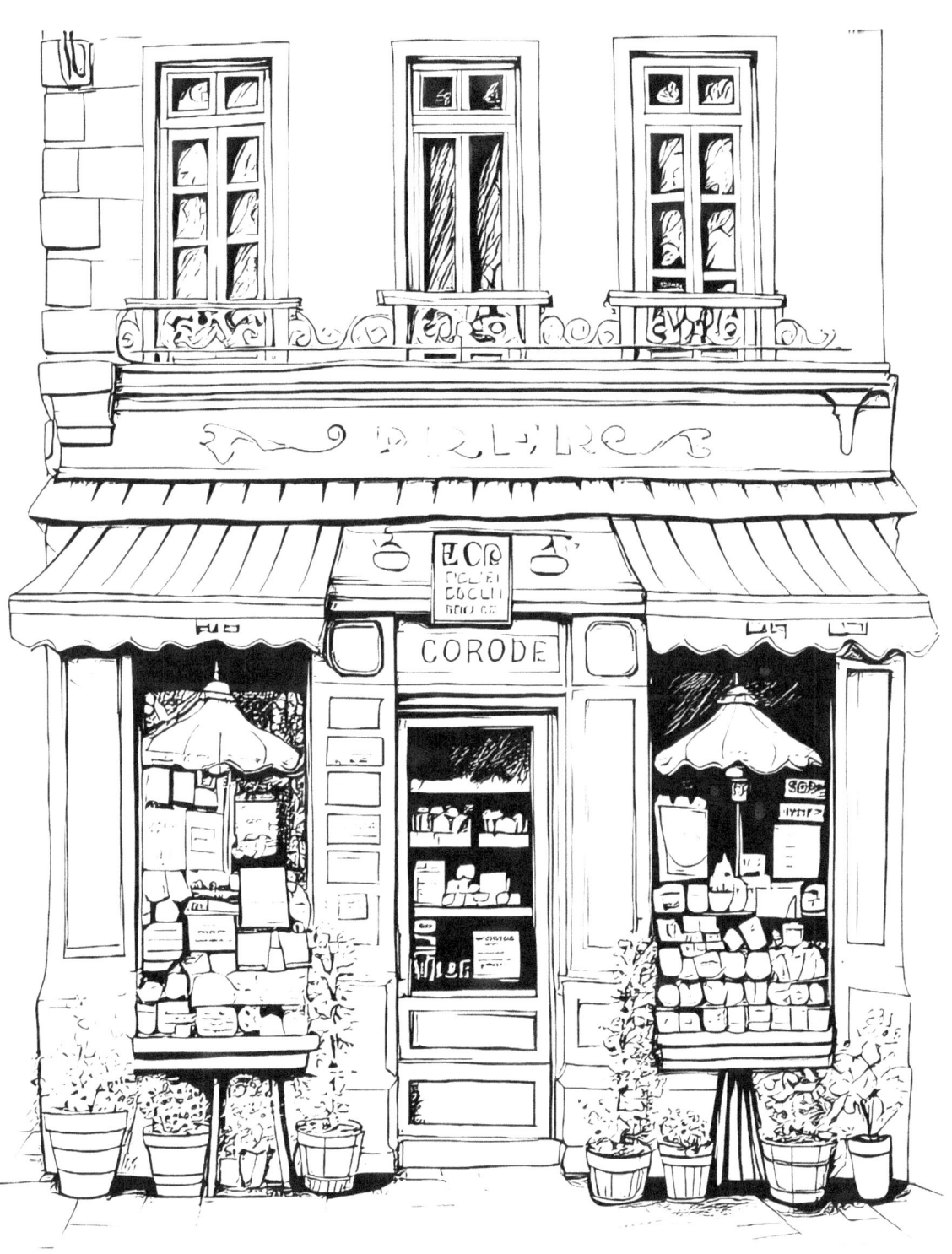

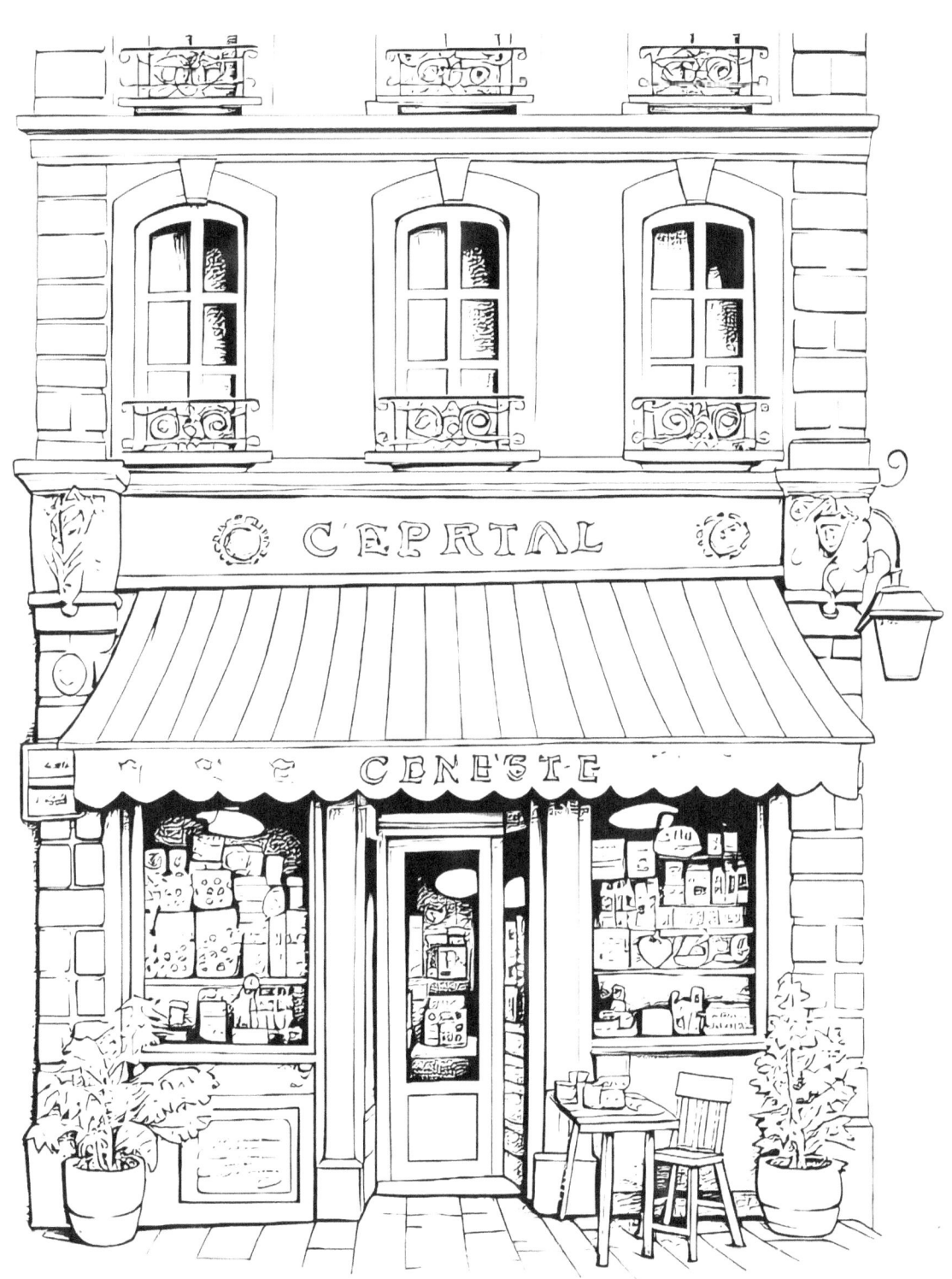

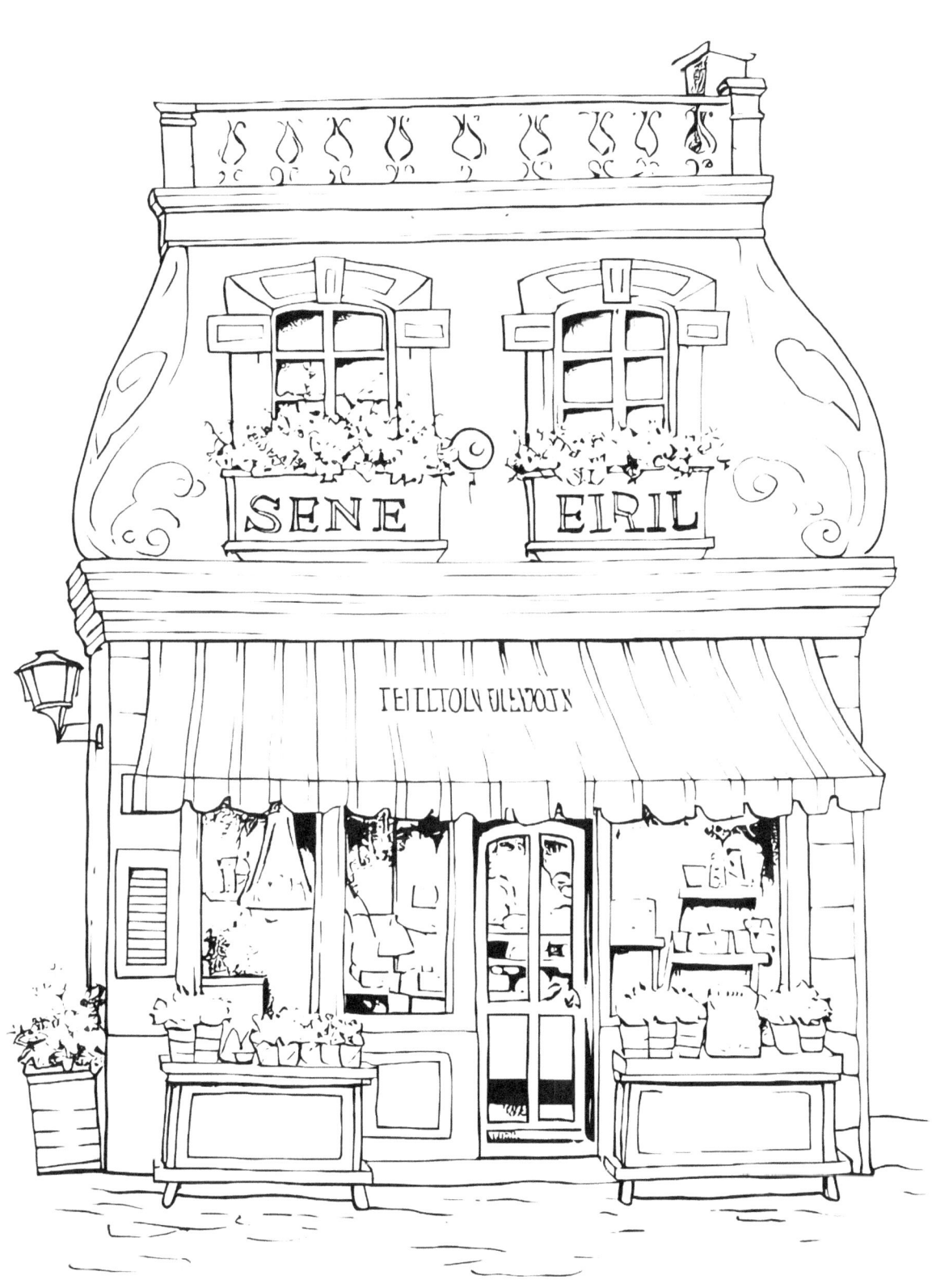

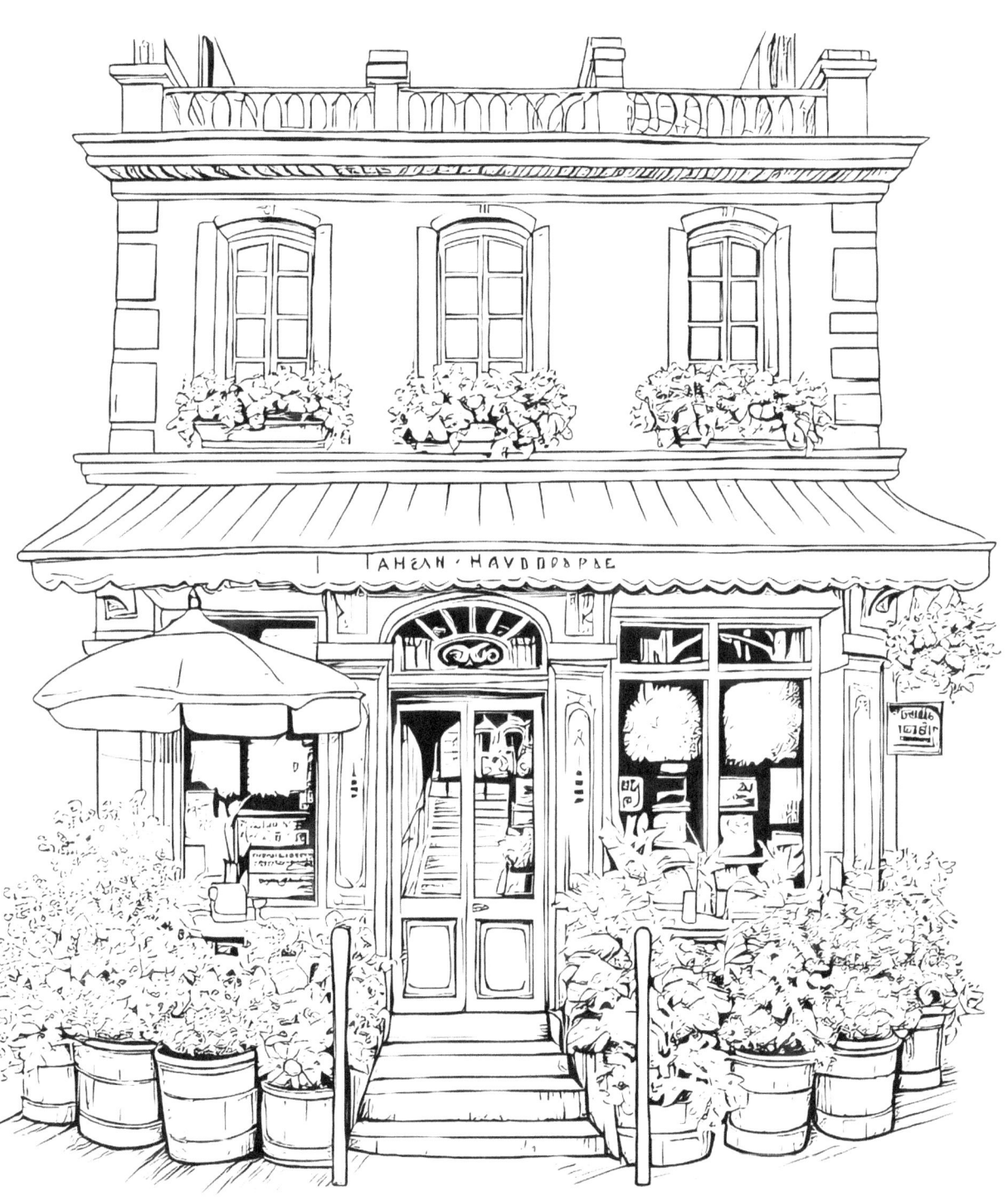

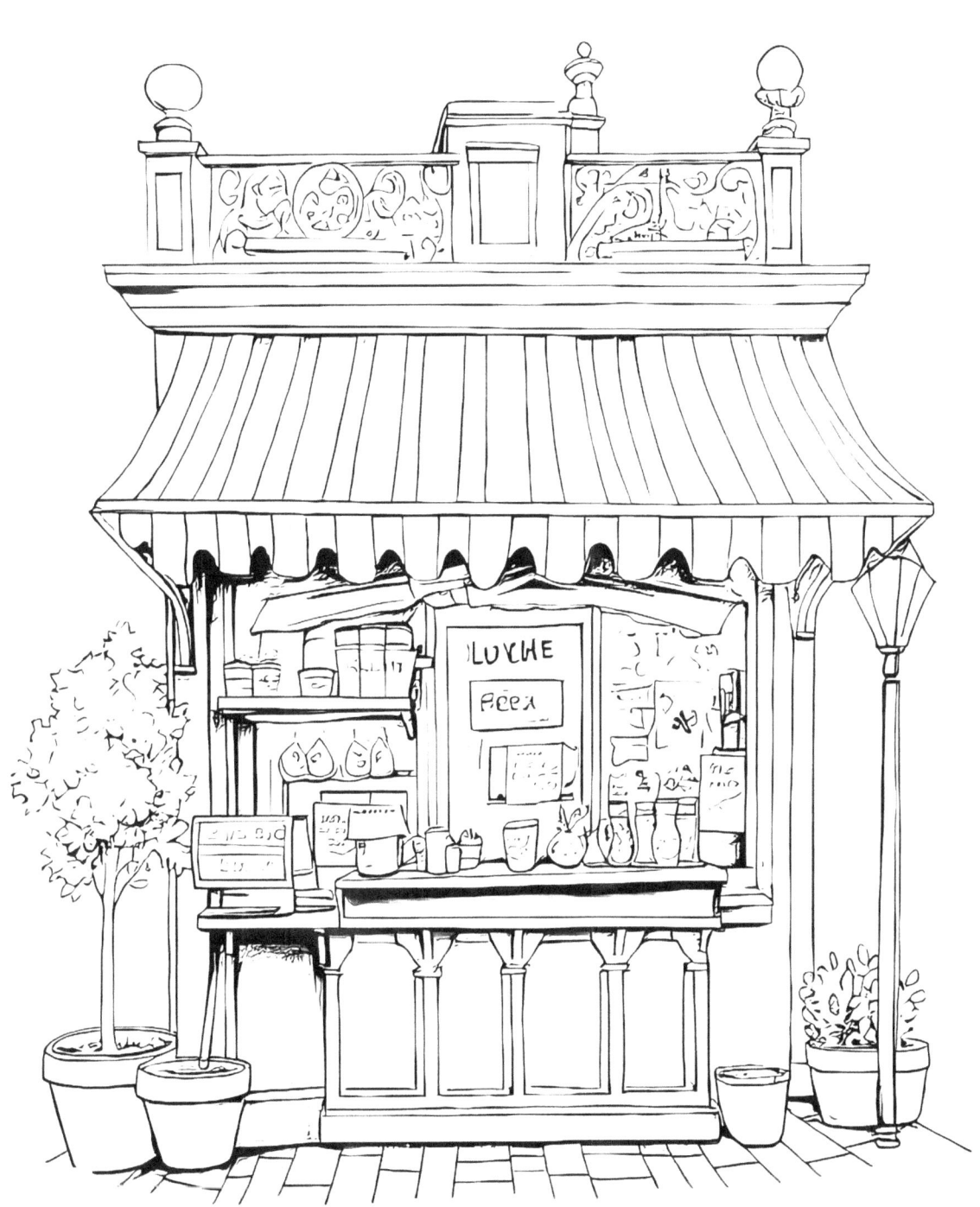

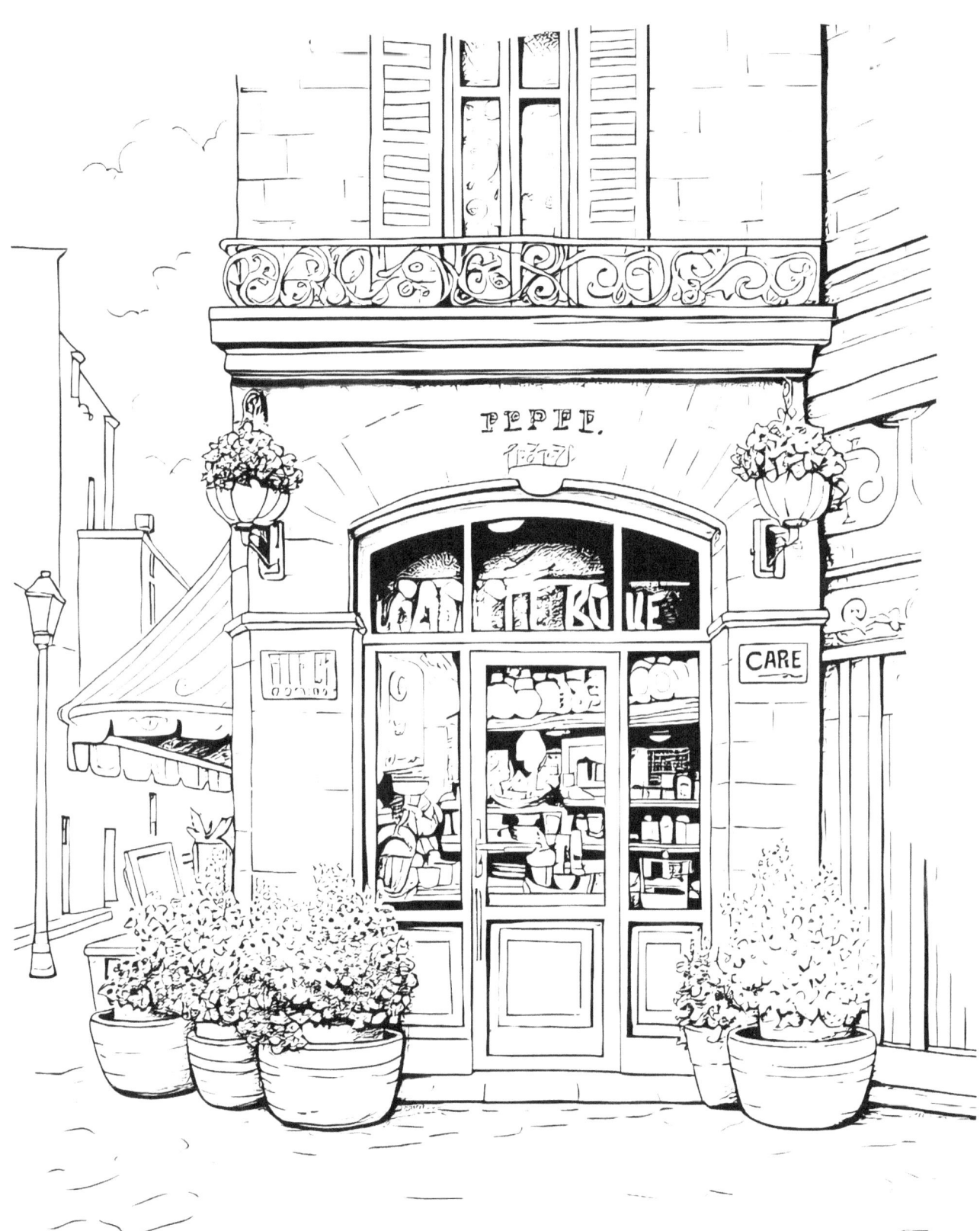

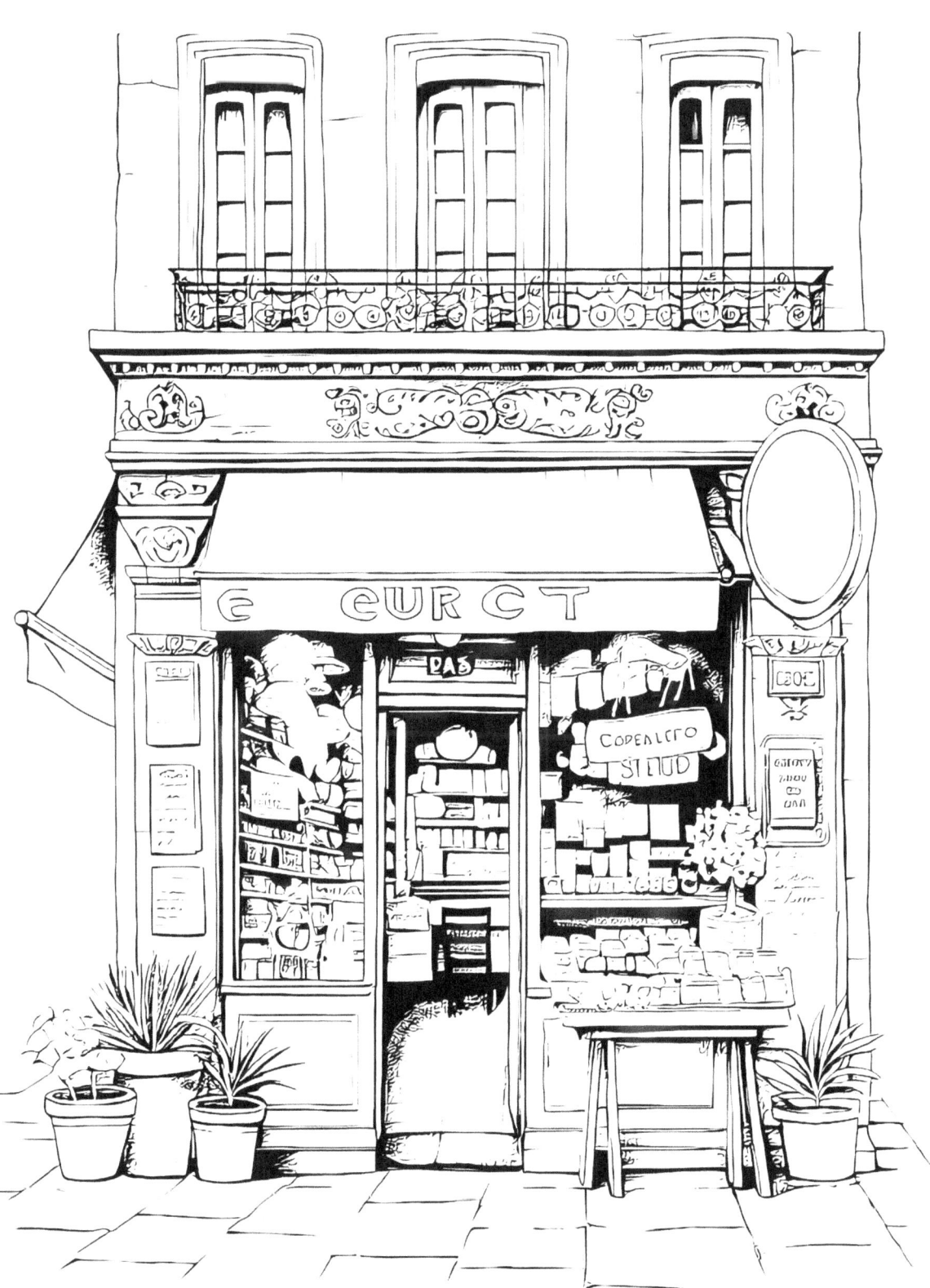

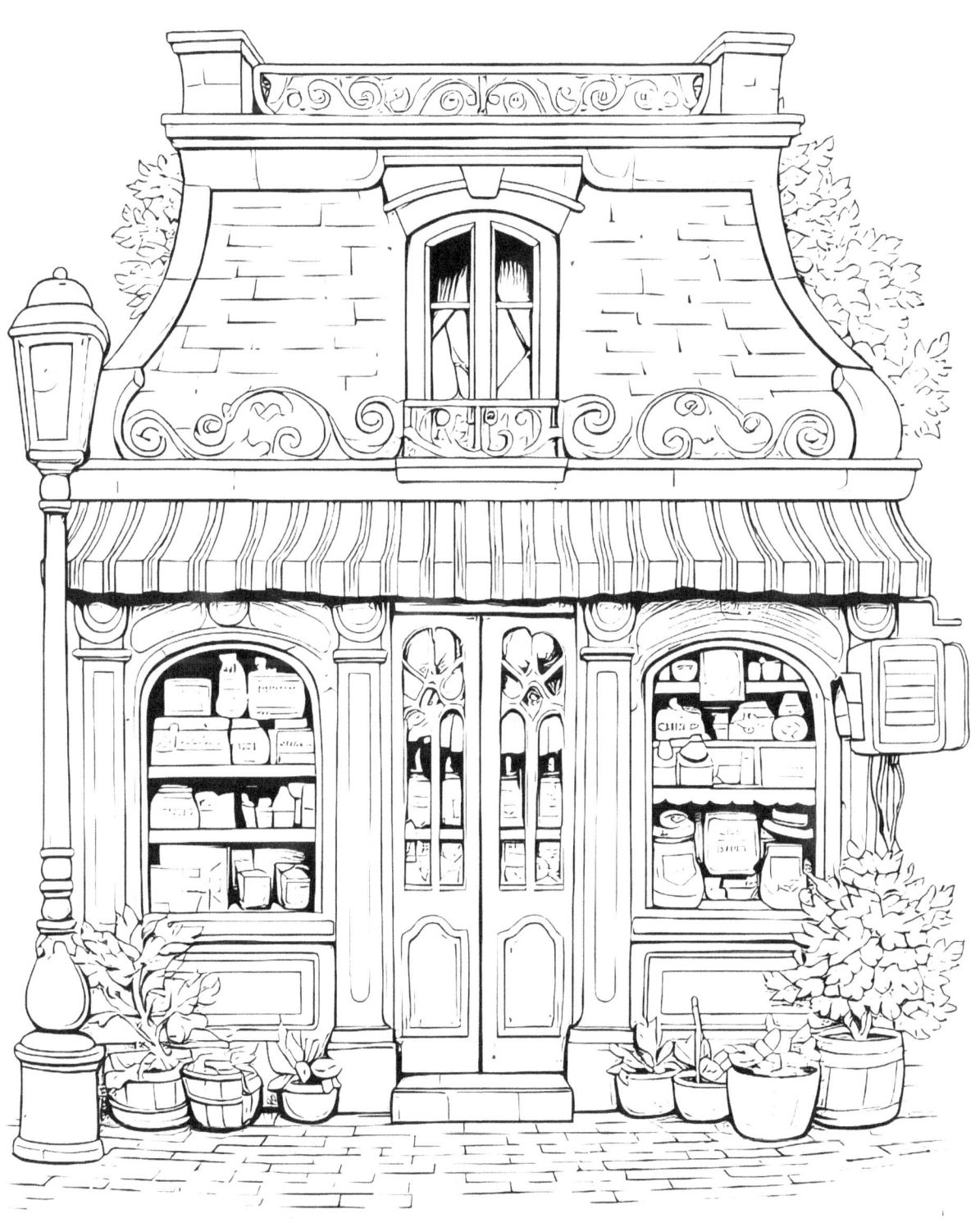

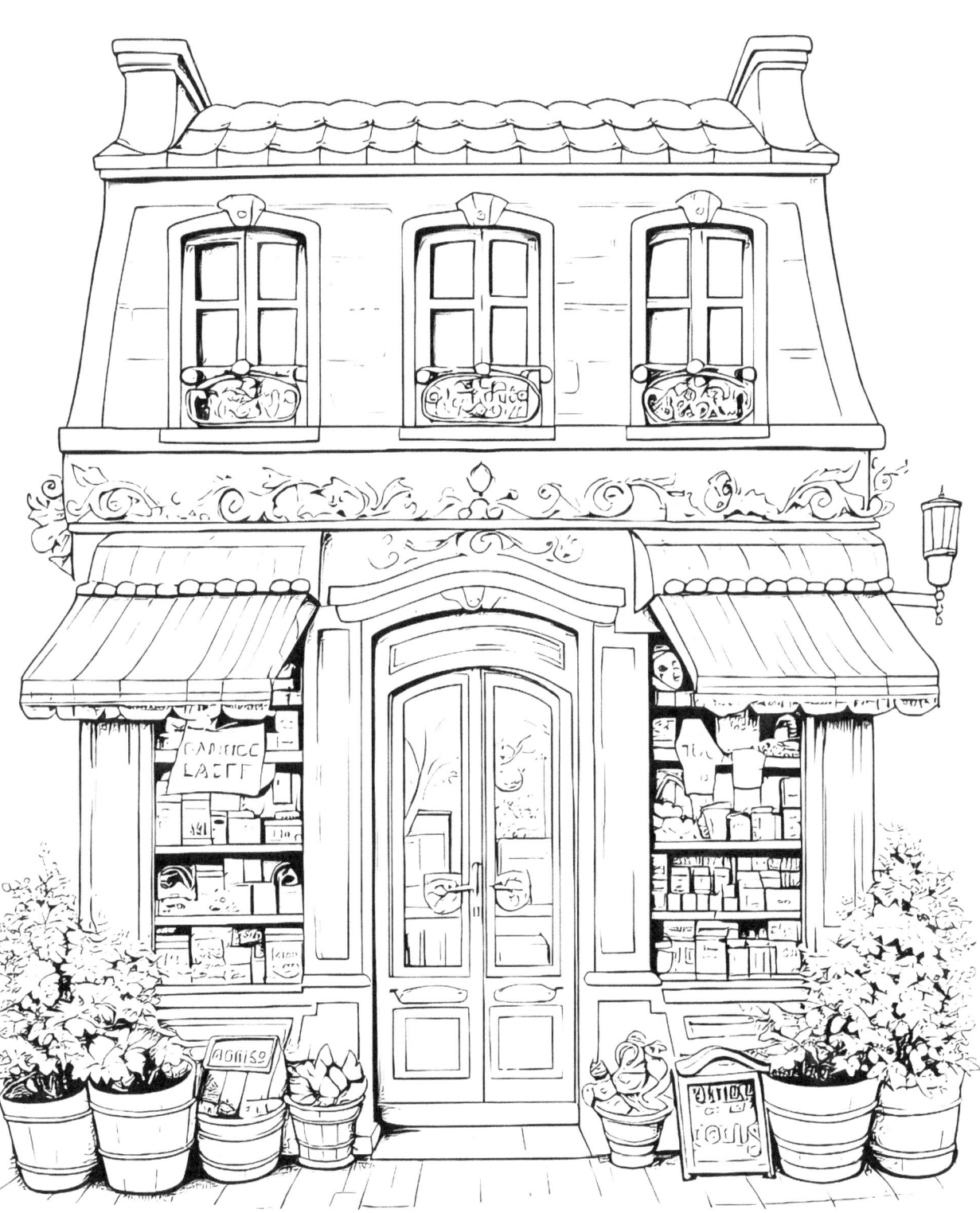

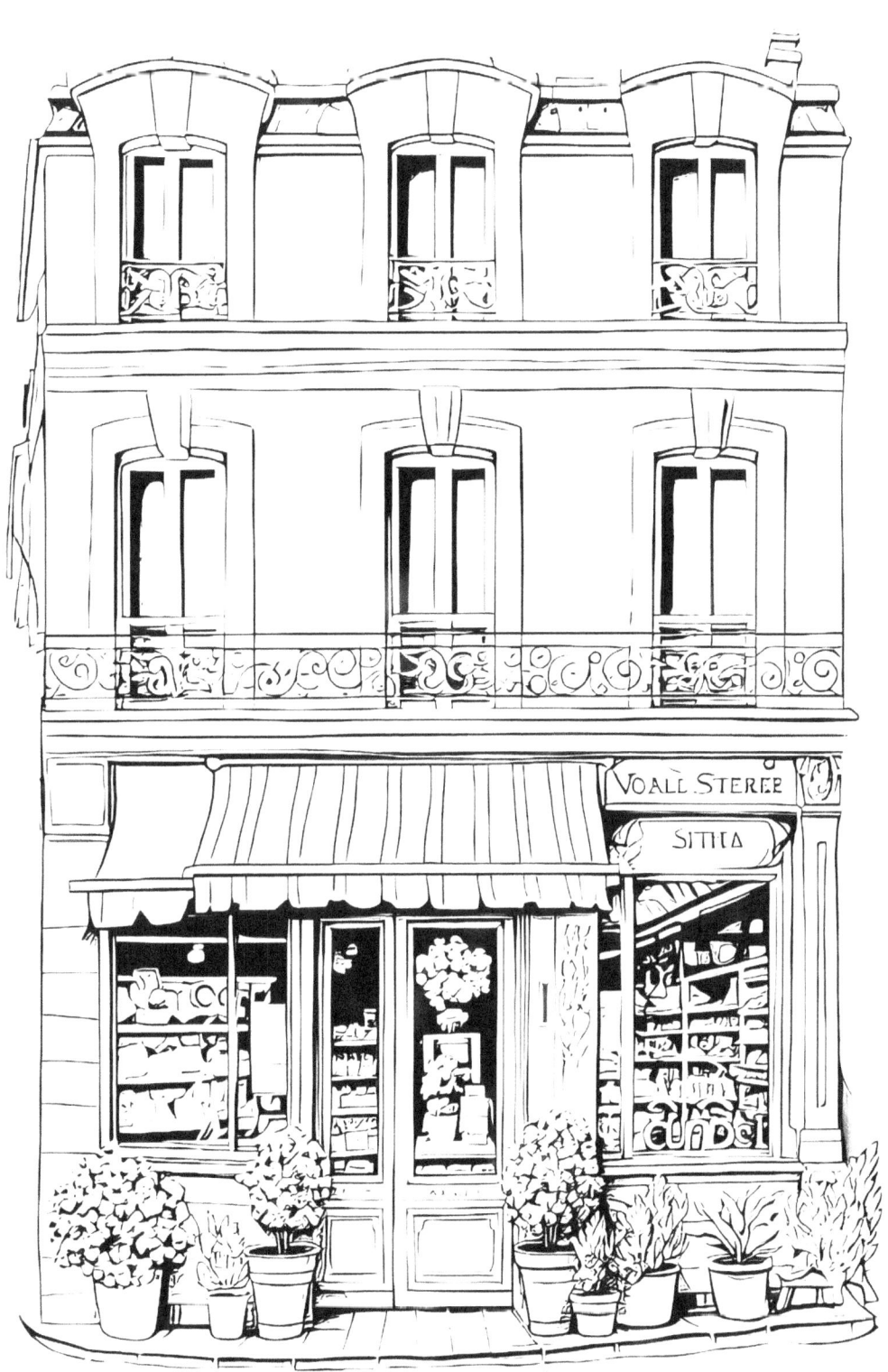

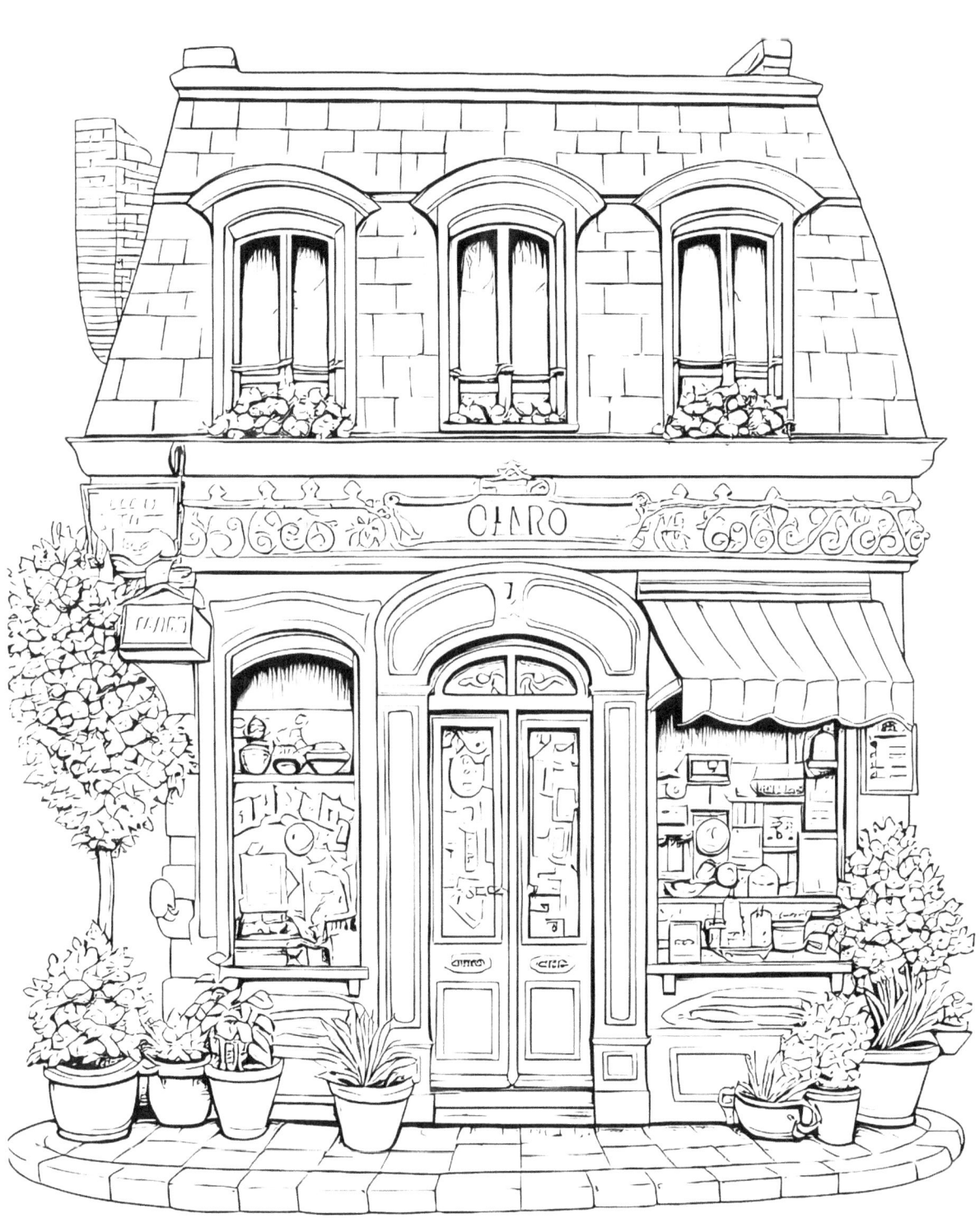

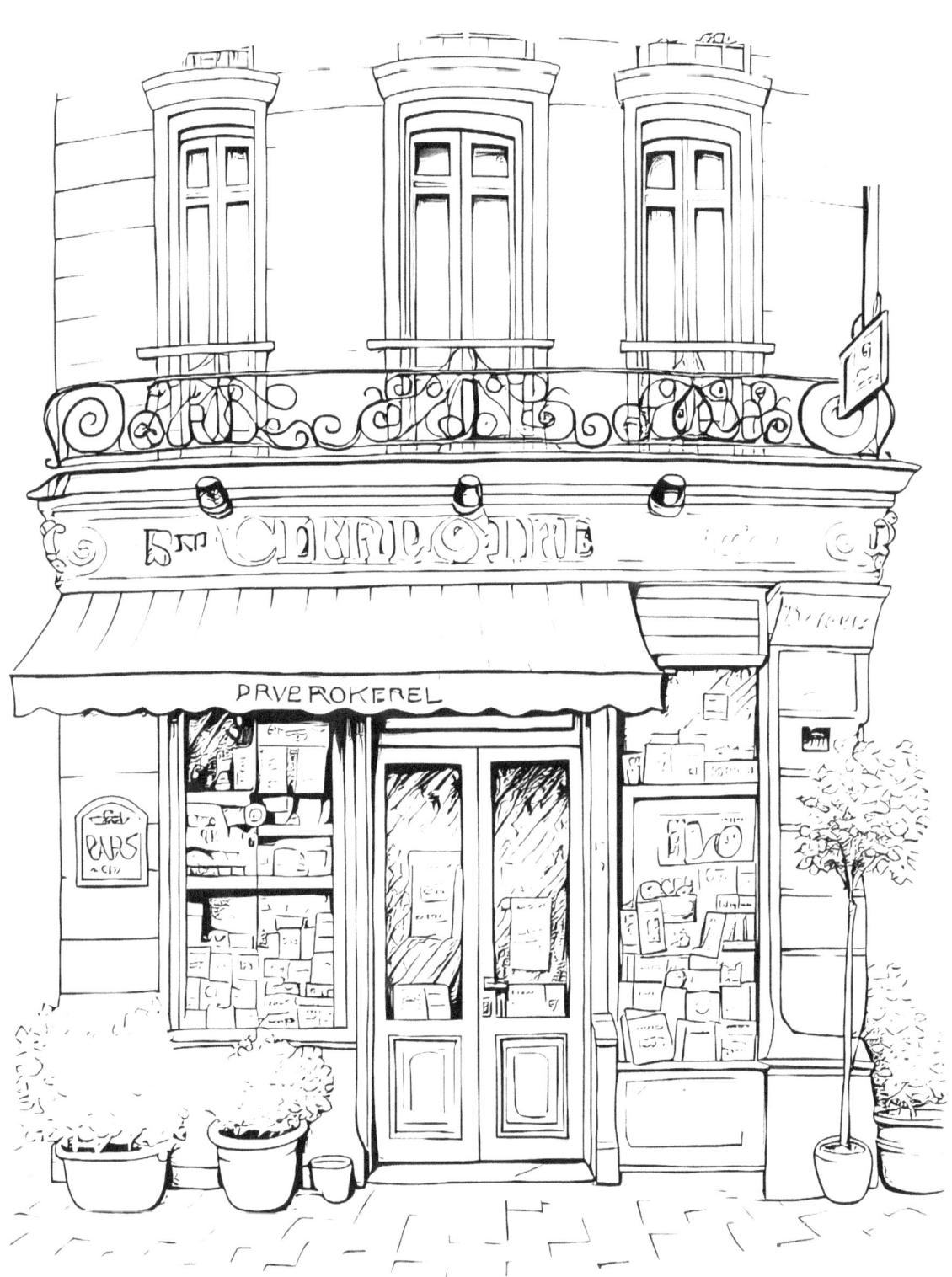

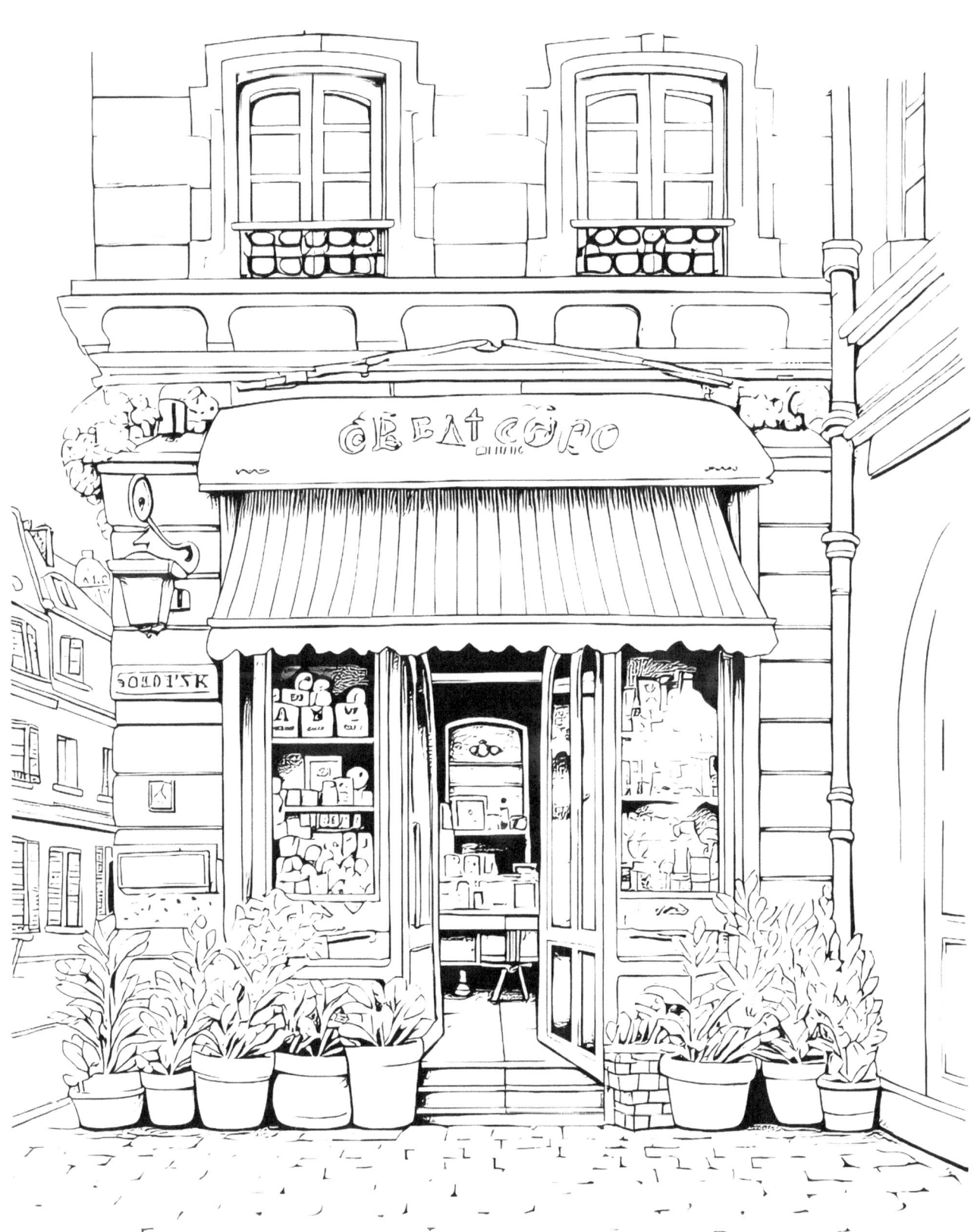

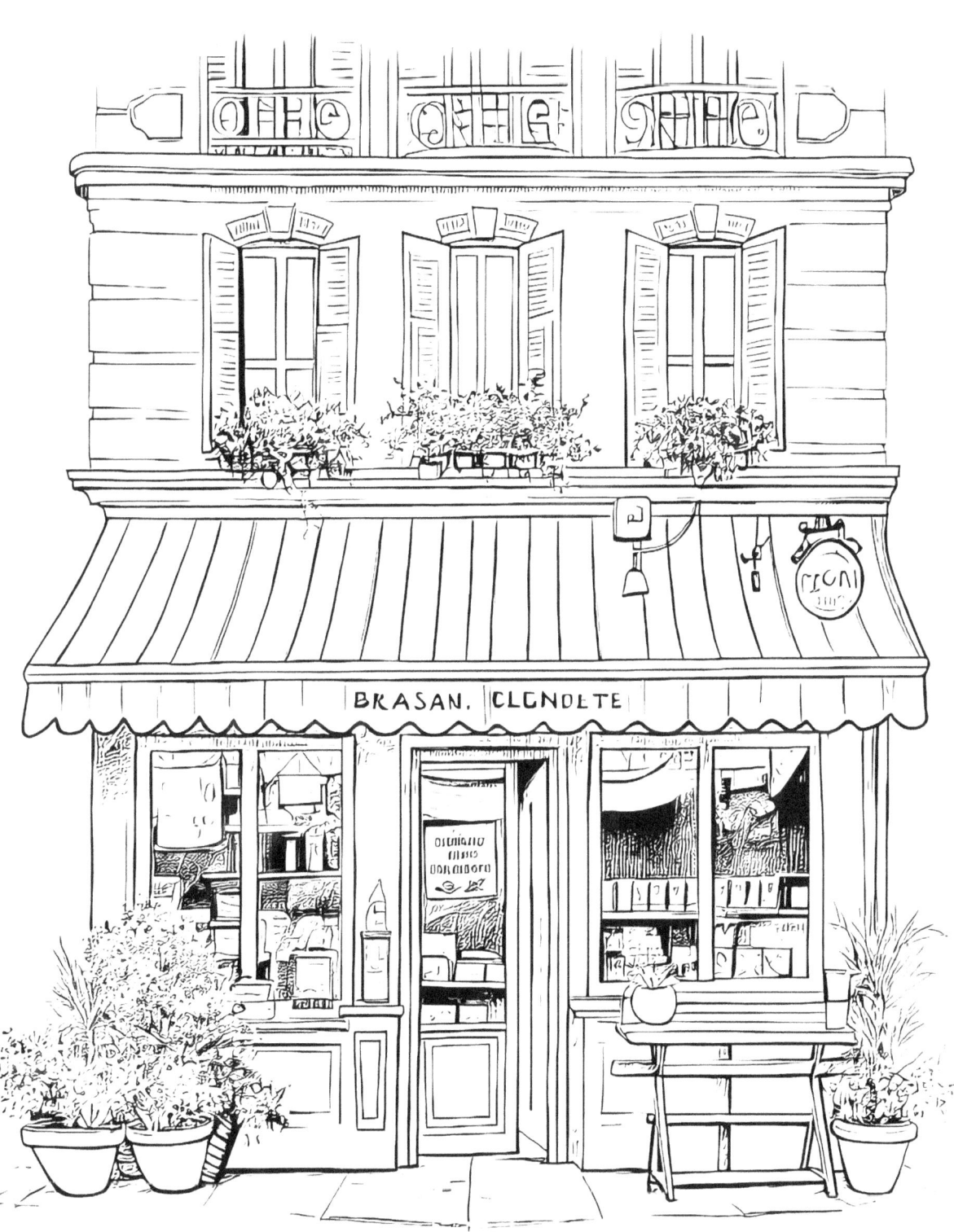

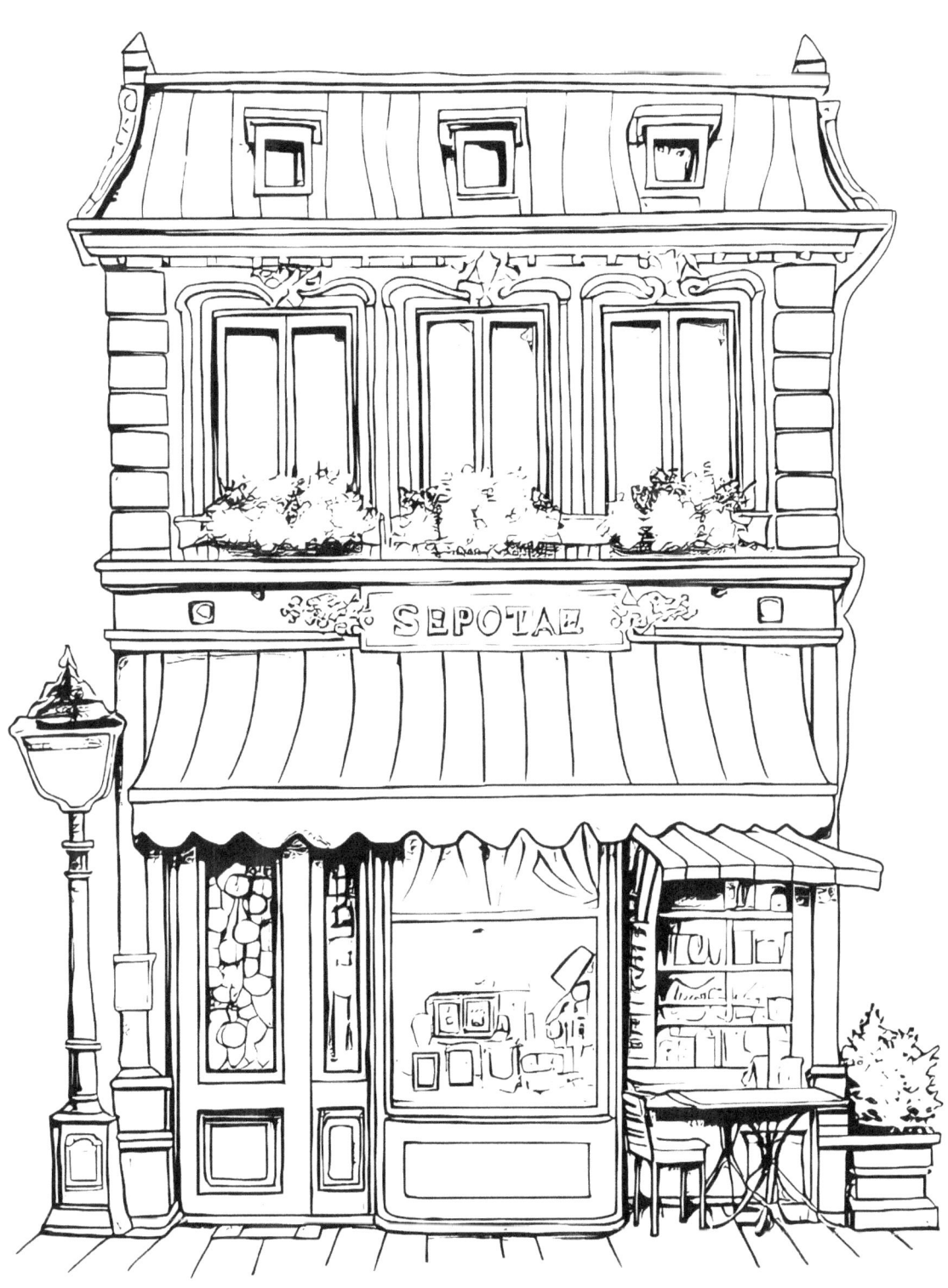

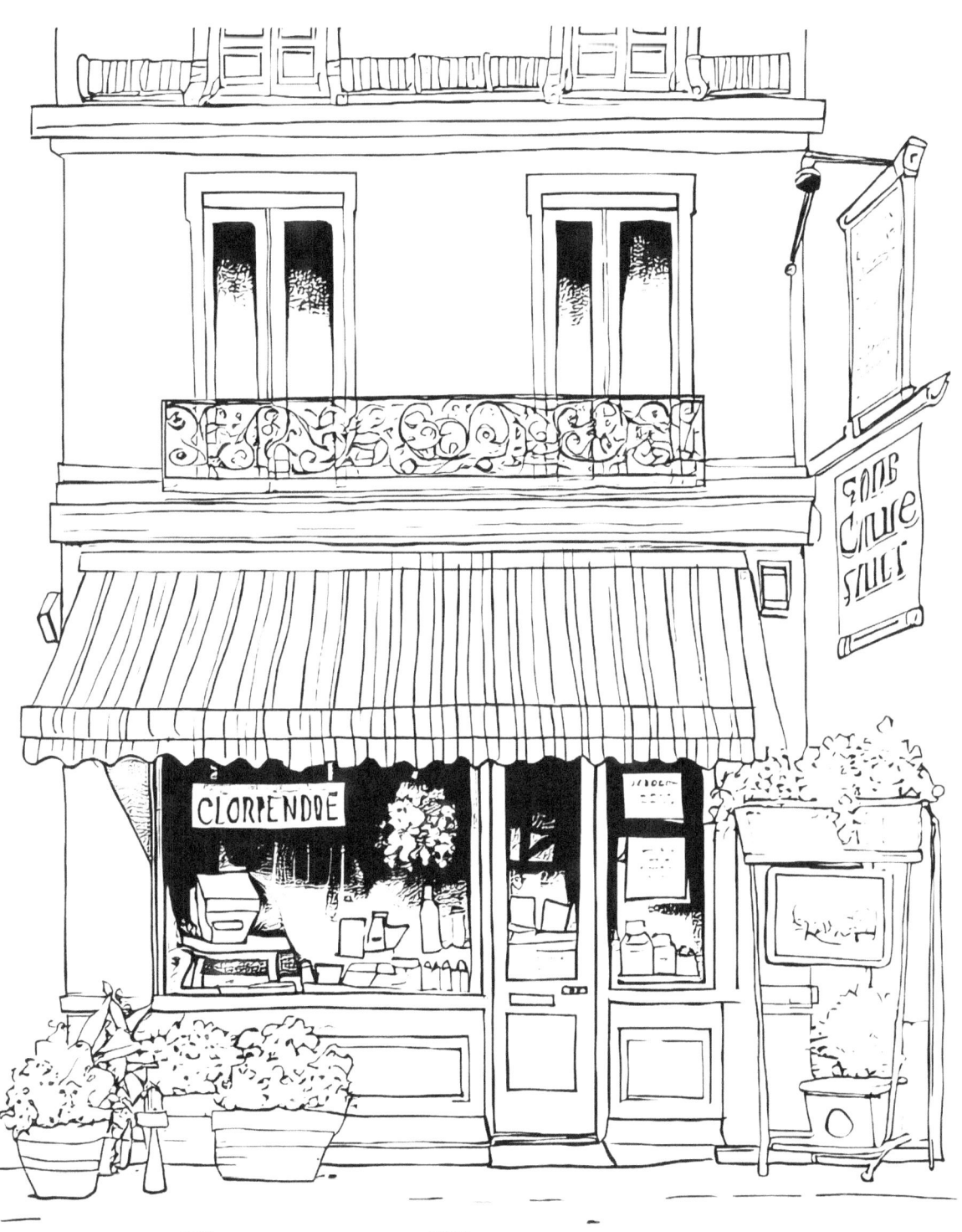

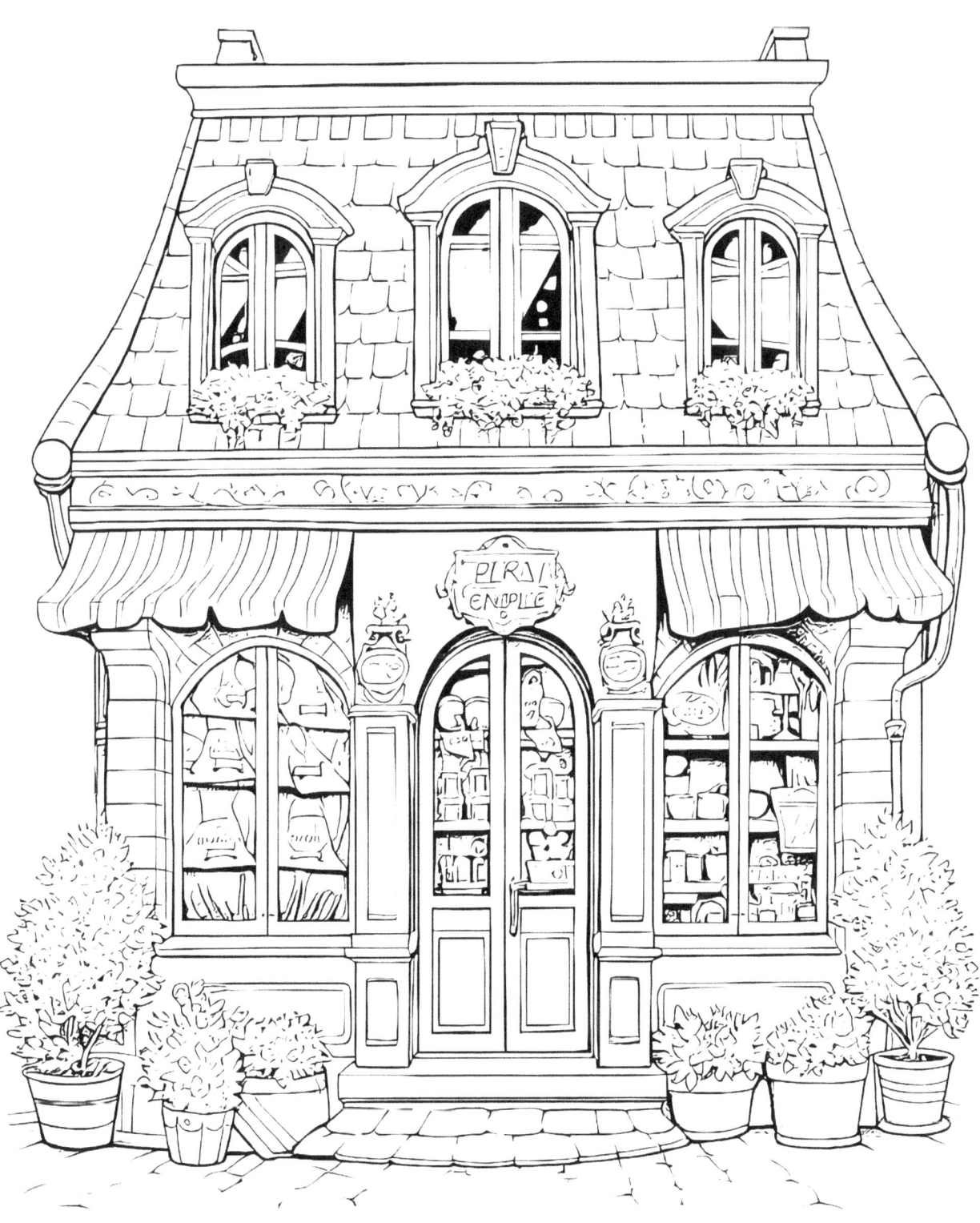

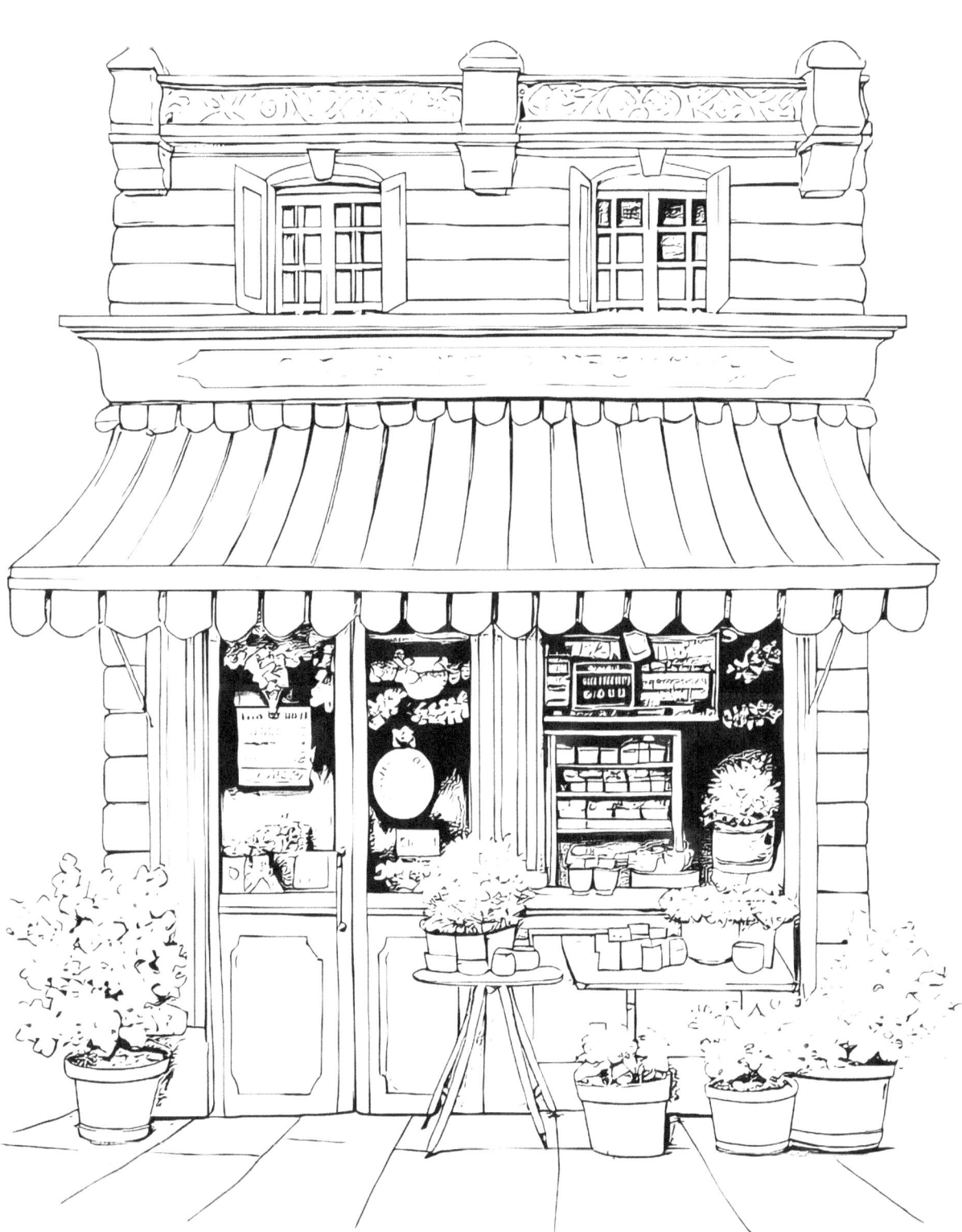

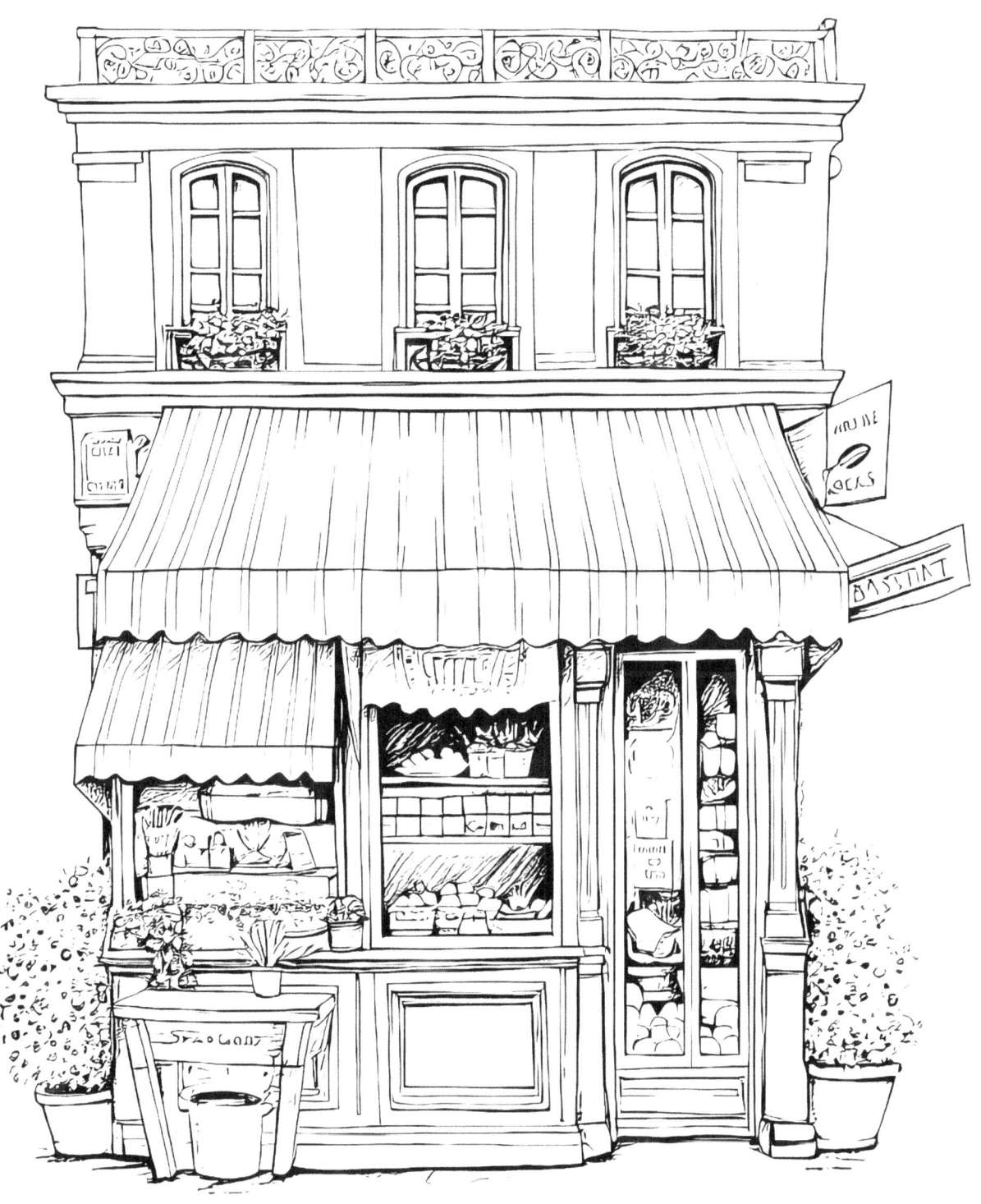

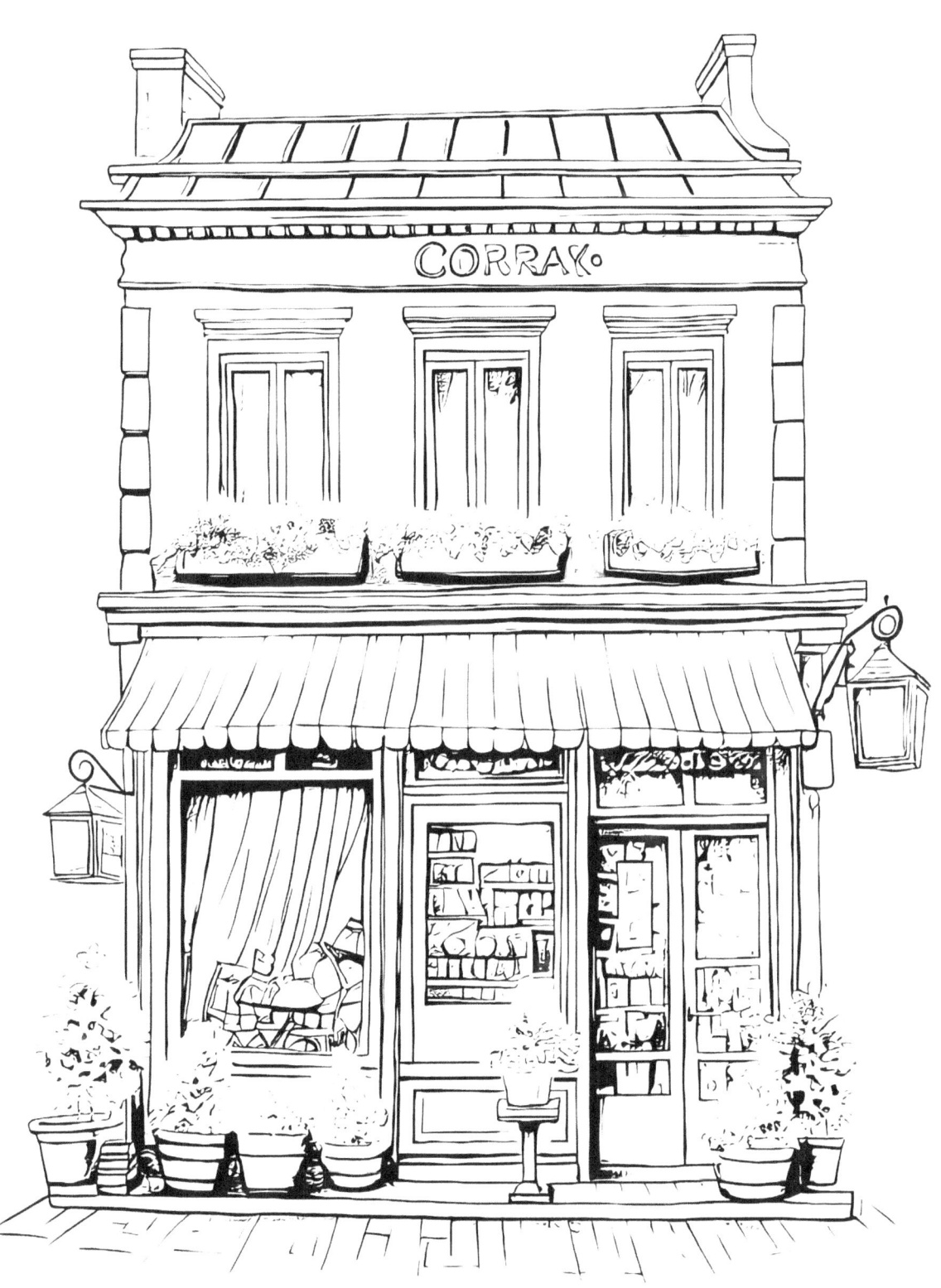

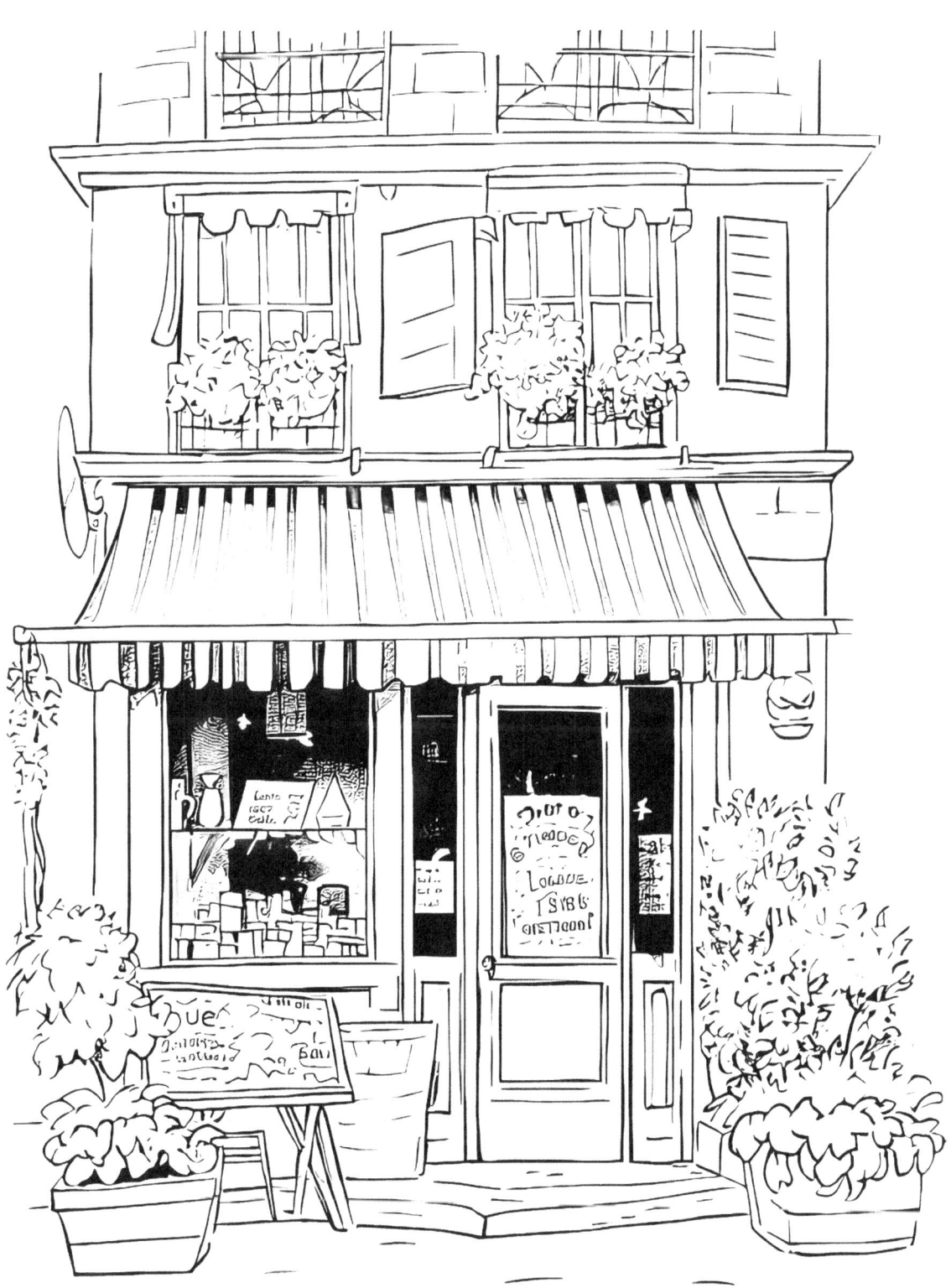

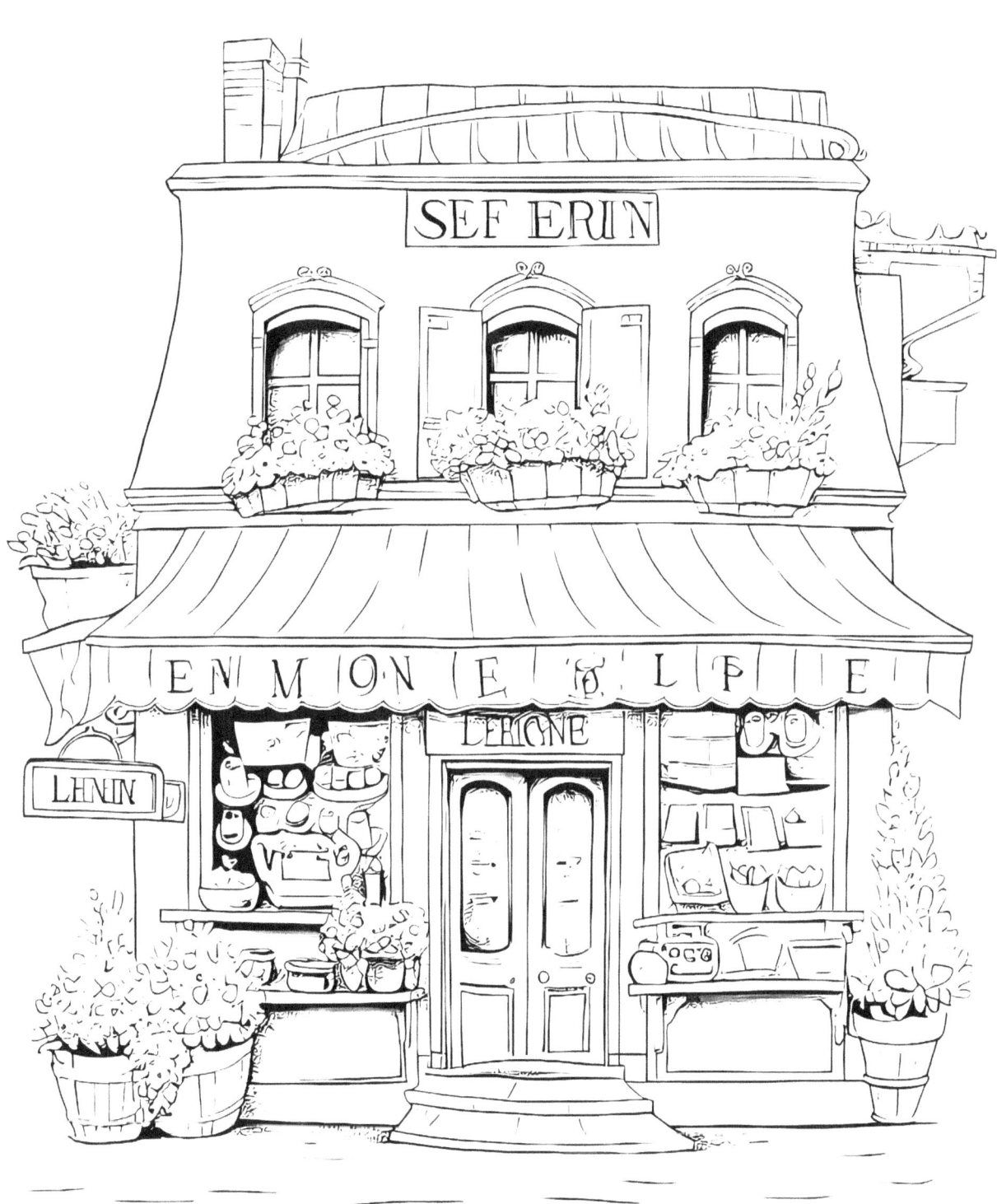

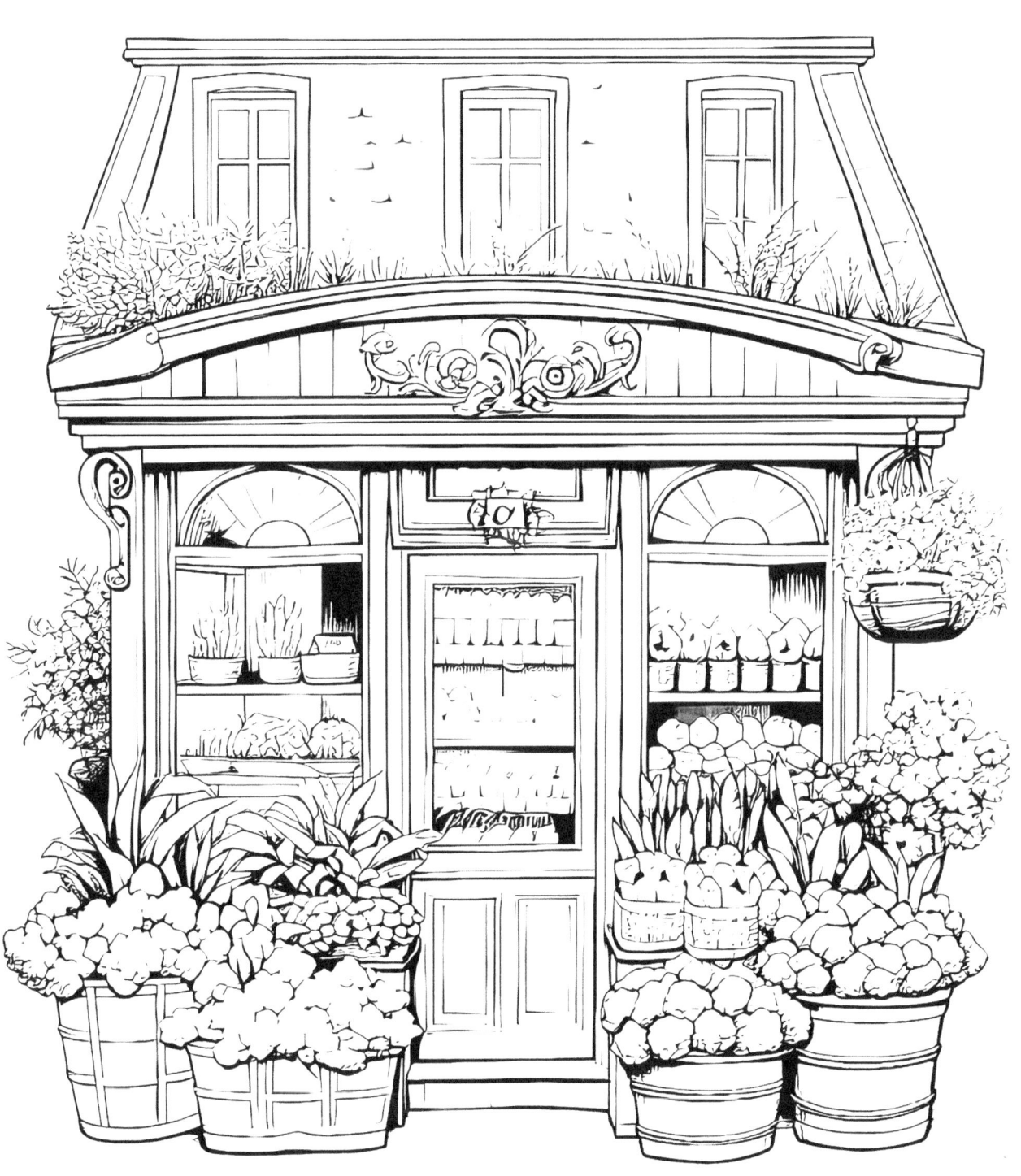

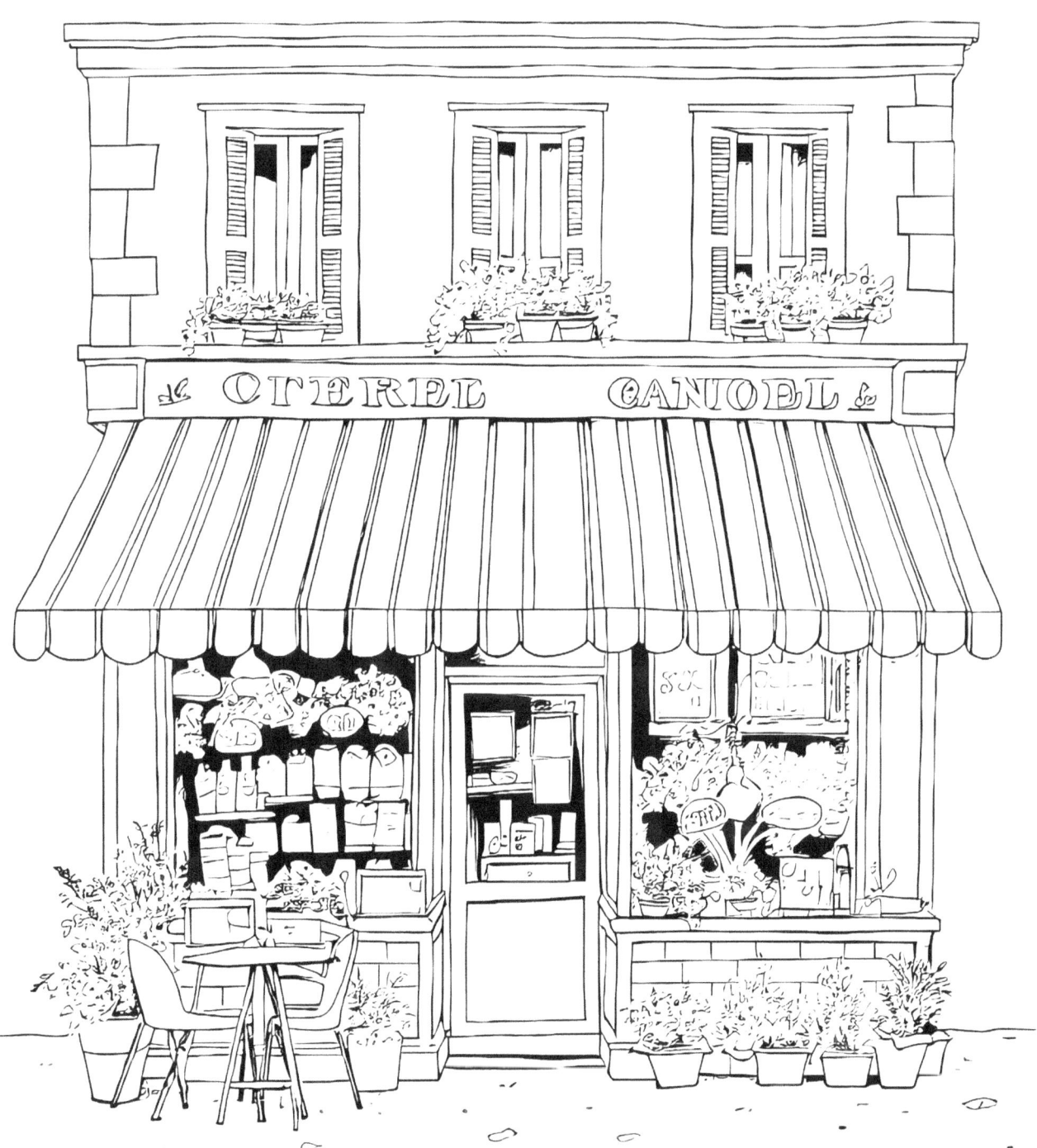

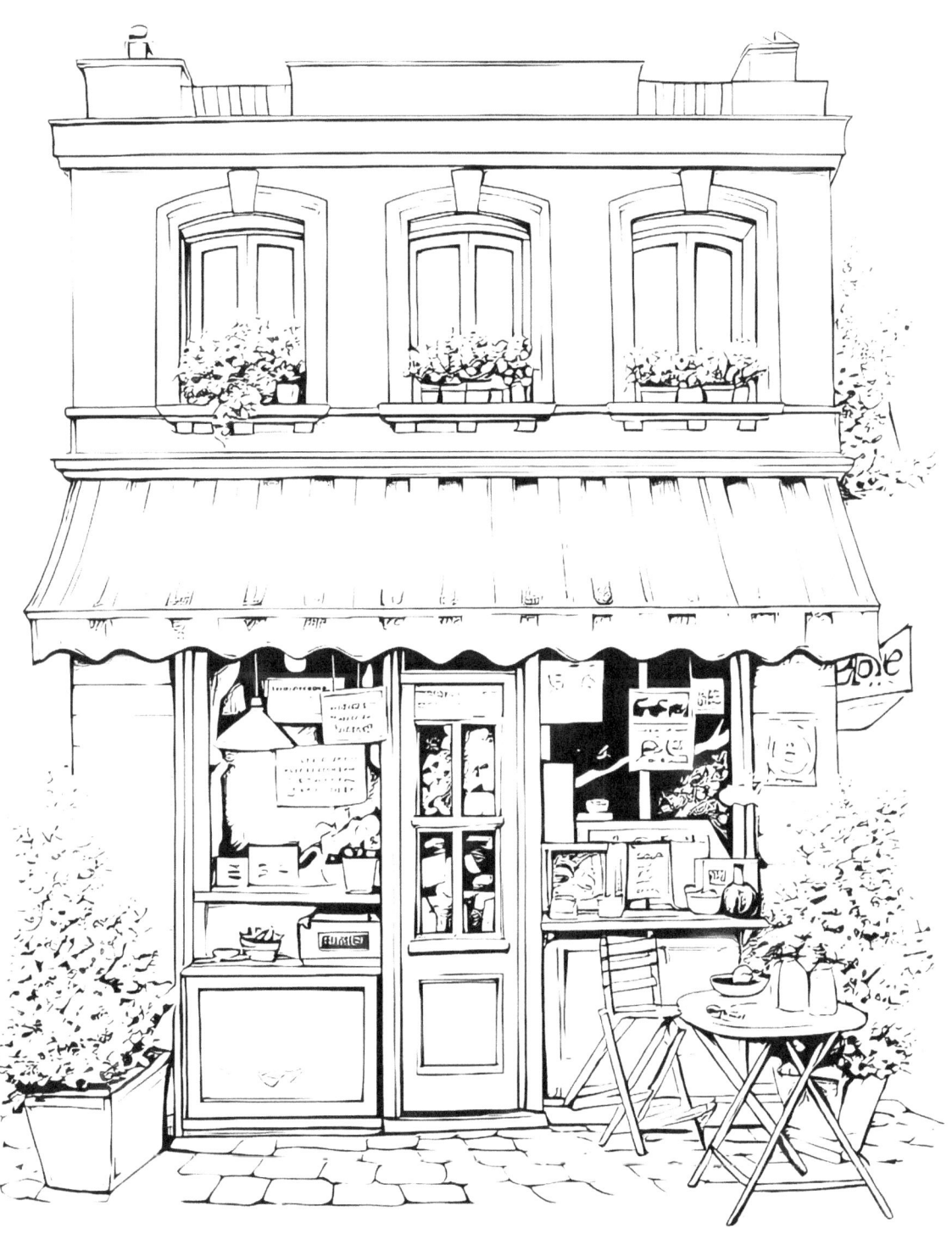

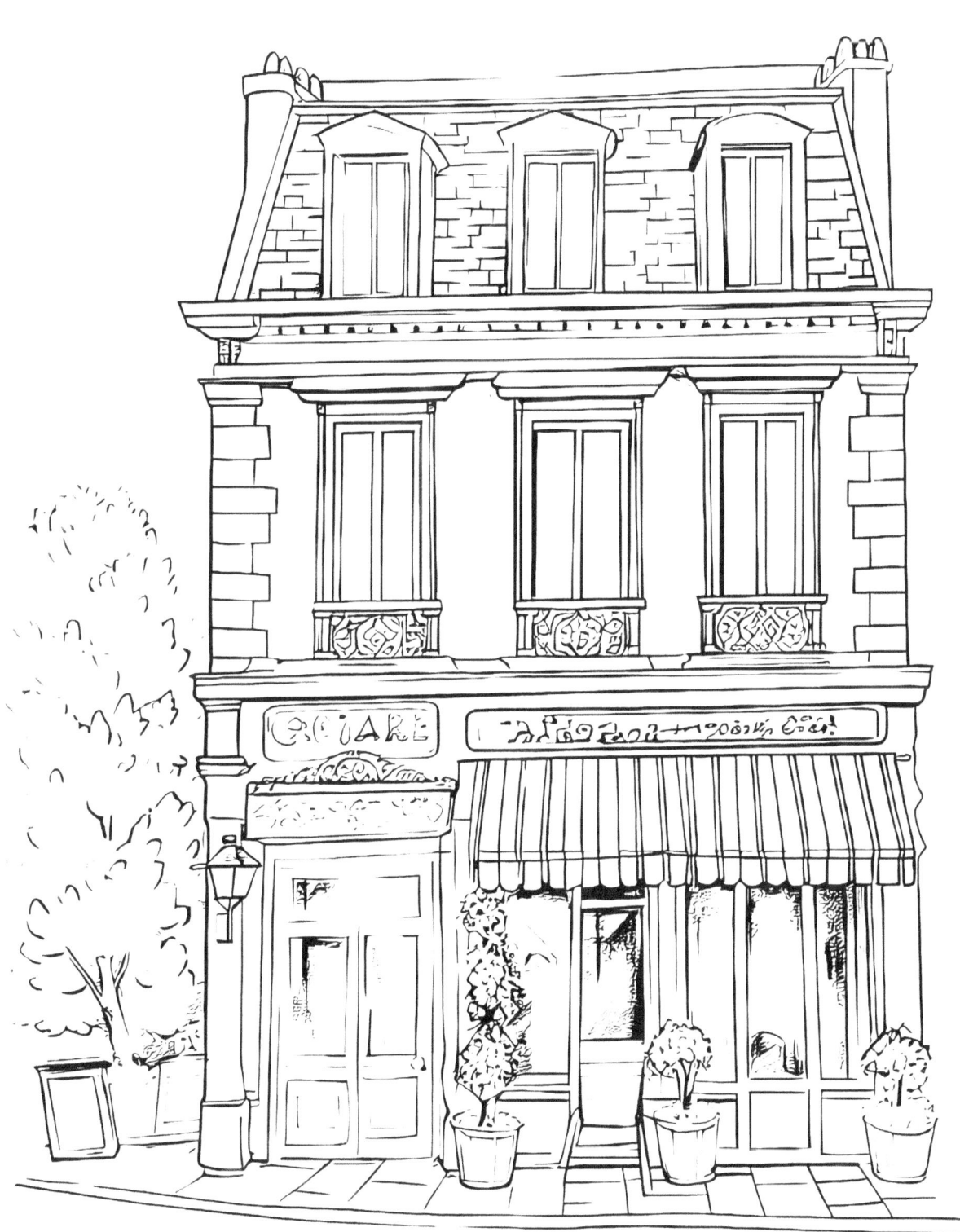

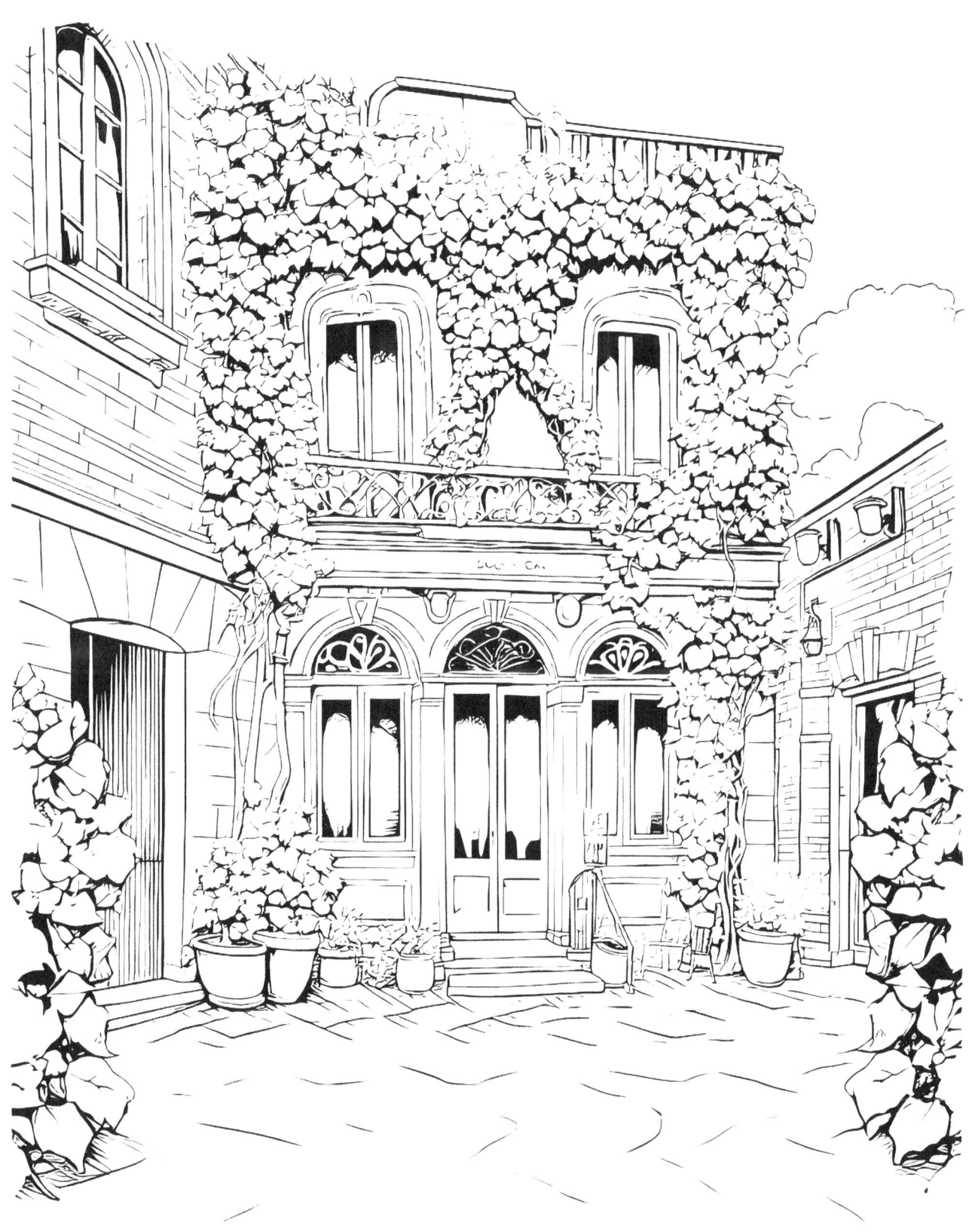